Kids Write Through It

Kids Write Through It

ESSAYS FROM KIDS WHO HAVE
TRIUMPHED OVER TROUBLE

Compiled by the editors at Fairview Press

Fairview Press

MINNEAPOLIS

Published by Fairview Press, 2450 Riverside Avenue South, Minneapolis, MN 55454.

Library of Congress Cataloging-in-Publication Data
Kids write through it : essays from kids who have triumphed over trouble / compiled by the
    editors at Fairview Press.
        p.   cm.
        Summary: A collection of essays in which the writers relate how they have worked
    through problem situations such as illness, the death of a parent, or the loss of a pet.
        ISBN 1-57749-081-9 (pbk. : alk. paper)
        1. Problem solving in children--Juvenile literature. 2. Life change events--Juvenile
    literature. 3. Adjustment (Psychology) in children--Juvenile literature. 4. Children's
    writings, American. [1. Problem solving. 2. Conduct of life. 3. Behavior. 4. Children's
    writings.] I. Fairview Press.
    BF 723.P8K53   1998
    155.4'1824--dc21   98-37697
                                                                            CIP
                                                                            AC

First Printing: November 1998

Printed in the United States of America
02 01 00 99 98   7 6 5 4 3 2 1

Cover: *Cover Design by Laurie Duren™*

Publisher's Note: Fairview Press publications, including *Kids Write Through It*, do not necessarily reflect the philosophy of Fairview Health Services.

For a free current catalog of Fairview Press titles, please call toll-free 1-800-544-8207. Or visit our website at www.Press.Fairview.org.

Contents

Foreword ix

Preface xv

Acknowledgments xix

TAKING CHANCES, MEETING CHALLENGES

"Challenge," by Jacquelyn DeGrendele 3

"Stage Fright," by LorLa. 5

"Don't Drink and Drive," by Michelle Vetter 7

LOSS OF A PET

"Mittens," by Destinee Leigh Downey 13

"Molly," by Elizabeth Patrick 15

"How I Saved a Dog's Life," by Kate 17

DEATH AND DYING

"The Night My Sister Died,"
    by Tyler Gregory Abrahamse 21

"The Gift of Time," by Amanda Kowalski 24

"When It Rains, It Pours," by Cheryl Ann   27

"The Night of Sorrow," by Maren   31

ILLNESS AND DISABILITY

"Believing in Myself," by Joshua Jay L.   37

"My Hero," by Kari Jo Johnson   39

"Something Deadly," by Galen Halbart   42

"My Brother," by Chelsea L.H.   46

"I'm Starting to Like Life," by A.J.   48

"A Walk through the Valley of the
    Shadow of Death," by Amanda Moore   50

"Living with ADD," by C.M.S.   53

"Twelve-Year-Old with a Broken Leg,"
    by Marcus Fitzgerald   56

FAMILY

"My Parents' Divorce," by Austin   63

"Is Your Mom Having a Baby?"
    by Derek William Jannarone   65

"Adoption Can Be Hard," by TAH   67

SELF-ESTEEM

"Shy," by Molly Brooks   71

"A Difficult Time," by John B. Giorgilli, III   74

"Being Overweight," by Jessica Haynes   77

PROBLEM RESOLUTION

"The Petition," by Nicole Starr   83

"Good and Bad," by K.T.   86

"A Smile Is a Sweet Reward," by Morgan Newton   88

"My Bike and Me," by Brian Osborne   91

"Too Much Pressure," by Alicia   93

SCHOOL

"First Day of School," by Jennifer   99

"Wrong School," by Zac Whitney   100

"Asking for Help," by Gill Carroll   105

DIVERSITY

"Friends," by Irene   111

"Aaron and Me," by Kelley Marie Oberne   114

Our Panel of Judges   117

Foreword

When I was a child, I talked like a child,
I thought like a child, I played like a child.
When I became a man,
I put away my childish things.

—*1 Cor. 13:11*

THIRTY YEARS AGO, THIS SIMPLE BIBLICAL QUOTATION caught the attention of an entire, chaotic generation. The country was in great turmoil, and we looked for validation wherever we could get it. Socially and politically conscious folks were drawn to the quote's irony. Academics called it insightful. Spiritual and religious types called it profound.

On one point, however, they were unanimous: The call to "put away childish things" meant making the transition from childhood to adulthood, leaving behind the thoughts and ways considered meaningless in the serious world of grown-ups.

The quote reflected a strong cultural belief that a child's life was an unfettered collection of games, fantasies, and creations. Children's friendships, it implied, were forged from mud, paints, and crayons. With nothing to do but play and go to school, kids were free from the problems that burden the adults around them.

Of course, we were so captivated by the wisdom of putting away our childish things that we missed the errors in our assumptions.

Children's lives are not nearly as carefree and blithe as conventional wisdom would have us believe. Many children have problems that rival those of adults, yet we sometimes fail to see how serious those problems can be.

Children ride the same emotional roller-coaster as adults, and they, too, rely on trusted relationships to help them through life. They look for and are receptive to love and support (even though it doesn't always look that way), and this leaves them open to hurt and disappointment. They bump into problems that are different or new; sometimes they become afraid.

As a culture, we pride ourselves on seeing children as "our most precious resource," but we fail to treat them that way. In order for a resource to make a contribution, it must first be credible. But credibility is something we rarely bestow upon children. Instead of validating them, we try to talk them out of what they think, know, feel, and believe.

Children are intuitive. They know when they're not being believed and when their experiences are being discounted.

Nevertheless, this process of invalidation is so intrinsic to adult-child relationships that it happens beyond the range of adult awareness. We don't even know we're doing it. While our intentions are usually honorable, the results often are not.

For example, when we try to calm a child's fears, we usually end up saying something like, "Oh, come on now, you're such a big girl, and there's really nothing to be afraid of!" Or "Look at Johnny! He jumped off the side of the pool—you can too!" Obviously our goal is to assuage a fear that prevents the child from taking on a new challenge. But when we try to talk a child out of his or her fear, we fail to get at the core of that fear. Instead, we leave the child with the sense that there is something wrong with him or her for feeling afraid in the first place.

Another example of good intentions gone wrong often occurs when we try to help a child through some type of pain, be it physical, emotional, or psychological. A typical first reaction is to minimize the pain. "Oh, honey, it's just a little cut—it can't hurt that bad! You're lucky it wasn't worse. At least you don't need stitches!"

When it comes to a child's disappointment, we do the same thing. The most common response is to try to lessen the disappointment or make the child believe that it wasn't such a big deal to begin with. "It was just a part in a silly old play. So you didn't get the lead. You still got a pretty good part! Look at it this way—not so many lines to memorize."

In each of these cases we expect children to figure out a way to skip over the bad stuff, "pass GO," and move directly into feeling better without having to slog through the muck. But our efforts to be supportive are hollow. It's tough to be helpful if we don't first acknowledge the child's perspective and trust his or her view.

Fortunately, things are slowly changing. Over the past several years, there has been an attempt to understand the complexities of a child's life. Increased efforts to explore and validate children's perceptions help foster this cultural change.

The book you are about to read is a collection of short essays written by young children who have overcome a challenge in their life. The fact that the book even exists is heartening evidence that we are, indeed, beginning to take children seriously and to give them the credibility they deserve.

The book's value for both children and adults is clear. For children, it validates what they suspected all along— that their pain, fears, and troubles are all real, and that they have the strength to overcome them. For adult readers, the book offers a fresh, perhaps even challenging, perspective on the insight and wisdom of children.

KATHLEEN J. PAPATOLA, PH.D.

Kathleen J. Papatola, Ph.D., graduated from the University of British Columbia, Vancouver, Canada, in 1982. She is a Licensed Psychologist with fifteen years of clinical experience. In addition to her clinical work, Dr. Papatola consults with organizations, trains mental health providers, and engages in public speaking. She is the author of The Therapy Answer Book: Getting the Most out of Counseling *and writes a regular column on current psychological issues for the* St. Paul Pioneer Press' Opinion Page.

Preface

WHEN WE SPONSORED OUR FIRST WRITING CONTEST four years ago, we had hoped to provide a forum for young people to discuss how they had overcome difficulties in their lives. We had also hoped that the writing process might become part of the healing process. But we had not anticipated that these young writers would inspire so many other people—both young and old—to maintain their courage in times of trouble, to survive, and, ultimately, to grow.

Last year we announced our second writing contest, and the response has been overwhelming. Hundreds of essays have poured in from across the nation. Many of these essays were heartbreaking to read; all were inspirational. We were deeply moved by the extraordinary courage and resiliency of these young writers, and we applaud their success in the face of adversity.

These essays carry the voices of children who have met with some of the troubling issues that affect young people today. Learning disabilities, fear, illness, death, low self-esteem—they're all here.

In the winning essay, "Being Overweight," twelve-year-old Jessica Haynes writes, "There were days when I came home in tears and I wouldn't want to go to school the next day. I hoped and prayed every night that I would wake up thin." After struggling for years with the teasing, the name calling, and her low self-esteem, Jessica displays courage and wisdom that many adults would envy: "I realized that pills and starving myself were not the answer. Now I try to eat a healthy diet. I have learned to express myself. I'm a good person and I'm okay just the way I am."

In the second-place essay, "My Hero," ten-year-old Kari Jo Johnson is devastated when her brother Zach is born with Down's syndrome. She soon learns, however, that rather than tear her world apart, Zach's disability actually brings her family closer together. "It all started when Zach was born and I thought my life was ruined. Now, I wouldn't trade my life or my family for anything in the world. He is my hero, and I love him very much."

The third-place essay, "The Night of Sorrow," tells the heart-breaking story of a child who learns that her father has died. Twelve-year-old Maren writes: "It was late and the roads were slippery. As my father entered a tunnel, he swerved and hit a safety bar, which threw him into the back seat. He was wearing his seat belt, but the force was too strong. The police officer told my mom that in the last two seconds of his life he probably thought about two things: his wife and his children." Her family drew closer together after the tragedy, sharing memories and developing rituals to help themselves cope with their loss. "Over the seven years since the accident, I have overcome that horrible night. I think I have survived this tragedy well, and so have my mom and sister, whom I love very much. . . . I learned that things can happen unexpectedly at any time. Sometimes these things can really tear your world apart. . . . I very much understand kids who have lost a loved one at a young age, because I've been there."

Every writer in this book has a story to tell. They have confronted their challenges head-on, and they have found the courage to write honestly about their experiences and share them with the world. They have persevered through fear, pain, and sadness, and triumphed over the trouble in their lives. Let these young people be an inspiration to us all.

FAIRVIEW PRESS

Acknowledgments

FAIRVIEW PRESS WOULD LIKE TO THANK THE FOLLOWING organizations for their gracious support of this project. Without them, this book would not have been possible.

For their generous financial support, we would like to thank the Fairview Foundation. We would also like to thank:

Automated Mailing Corporation

Capital City Pride

Cold Side Silkscreening

DRAGnet

Hungry Mind Bookstore

Mall of America

Message! Products

Minnesota Vikings

Simek's

Soderberg Florist

SuperAmerica

Tiro Industries

Walgreens

For her special contribution to this project, we sincerely thank Kathleen J. Papatola, Ph.D.

We are also grateful to our panel of judges, whose time and effort have contributed so much to this book:

Mayor Norm Coleman of St. Paul
Marly Cornell, Fairview Health Services
Senator Rod Grams of Minnesota
Linda Hillyer of Massachusetts
Nkauj'lis Lyfoung, KTCA's *Don't Believe the Hype*
Kathleen Papatola, *St. Paul Pioneer Press*
Herticena Self of Minnesota
Robyn Freedman Spizman, TV's "Super Mom"

Finally, for the heart behind the book and the words within each story, we would like to thank all of the kids who sent in their essays. Though the final choices for publication were difficult, every essay we received contributed to this remarkable book. Thank you all, from Fairview Press.

TAKING CHANCES, MEETING CHALLENGES

Challenge

Jacquelyn DeGrendele, age 12

"BEEP" WENT THE LOUD SPEAKER AT SCHOOL. IT WAS A warm afternoon. I was sweating. The principal announced on the intercom, "Students, if you are interested in running for president of the student body, please go to Room 20 at lunchtime." I knew at that instant I wanted to campaign.

I was in fifth grade. That afternoon, I rushed to Room 20 and skidded to a stop right in front of the door. I straightened my shirt and brushed off my pants. My nerves were trembling. If I were to have spoken at that moment, my voice would have been shaky. I opened the door and stepped inside. As I took a seat by a window, I saw that I had many opponents. The room was crowded and everyone was giving indignant glares to each other, wondering who was the best, who would win. The teacher talked for a long time and then handed to each student a packet that thirty students, our teacher, and our parents had to sign.

I turned in my packet full of signatures. The next day, I had to give a speech. I had no idea what I should say. I sat in my chair in the full auditorium. When it was my turn, I climbed the four steps to the stage. It felt like there were one hundred steps instead of four. A million eyes were gazing at me. I had butterflies in my stomach. I cleared my throat and started my speech. I pronounced everything loudly and clearly, and when I finished everyone clapped. I was proud of myself.

After all the speeches, everyone went to their classroom to vote. I was afraid no one would vote for me. I looked around my class, watching my classmates as they voted. I wondered, Would I be the only one in my class checking Jacquelyn DeGrendele on the ballot? Warm drops of sweat dropped from my forehead to my nose, then onto the floor. I voted, turned in my ballot, and waited.

The next day, I jogged to the cafeteria to hear who won. I sat at a table and hummed to myself. The principal came and gave a speech. Finally, just when I thought I would burst, she announced the winner. I had lost. My stomach sank in disappointment. Yet, I tried to remain positive. I was sad I lost but felt glad I had tried. Campaigning was a lot of work, but it turned out to be a great learning experience.

Disappointment made me a stronger person, one who is willing to take risks and accept challenges. I learned that even when you try your best, sometimes you don't succeed. Still, you should try again.

Stage Fright

....

LorLa., age 12

I'VE BEEN THROUGH MANY PHASES AND CHALLENGES throughout my life. Still, most would say I am a rookie and the hardest times have yet to come.

For twelve years, I've lived with a loving family of five. I've accomplished what I thought I would fail at, and failed at what I thought I could accomplish.

When I was eight, I entered a city pageant. I had no knowledge at the time of what a pageant consisted of. Still, I followed the lead of the choreographer and tried to keep up.

Along with the other contestants, I prepared a speech about myself and why I wanted to represent our city as Junior Miss Coon Rapids. The pageant required a talent of some sort, anything from tap-dancing to playing an instrument.

My talent was singing, and I prepared an entertaining yet appropriate piece.

I came in as runner-up. I was proud of myself. Knowing I did my best and had a good time was a reward in itself.

The next year I tried again, hoping to win. When it came time to present my speech, something unexpected happened. I freaked. I was overcome with stage fright. With tears in my eyes and a scratchy voice, I wanted to go home and hide under the covers. My mom explained to me in a hurried manner that if I didn't go out there I'd mess up everyone's timing and the order of things in the pageant.

Reluctantly, I gave my speech, left the spotlight, and tried to regain my composure for the next event. After an hour, I had calmed down. This was my first experience of stage fright, and I overcame it by returning to present my talent. By the way, it went great!

The following year, we moved to a nearby city. There I went to a new school, made new friends, and basically started my social life over. Making new friends and leaving the old was a difficult thing to do, but with phone calls and visits every so often, the challenge was overcome.

My advice is this: It's hard to be prepared for everything. Sometimes you need to take life as it comes. And it's not a bad idea to have a good joke to tell in those stressful moments life gives us.

Don't Drink and Drive

Michelle Vetter, age 12

I'M NOT WRITING ABOUT A PROBLEM I HAD TO TACKLE, but instead about something I find inspirational, sad, and uplifting at the same time.

"Michelle, get up. My game starts in an hour," I heard every morning from my sister. I got up one morning to find a rainy, cloudy day, but they play softball in anything. My sister plays on a travel team that goes all over Ohio and has tournaments across the United States. We were in Toledo this morning. It was the playoff game. The team had never made it this far before.

Normally, I would be off with my friends Linsey, Chad, and Drew, but this time we were all watching the game. The score was tied—six to six—and the lead hitter from our team, Christy, was up to bat. The bases were loaded, with one out. She hit two runs in and the game was over. Everyone was so excited. We ran out onto the field to give her a hug. The team got trophies and certificates. That weekend was a blast. I felt really happy for Christy.

My sister went home with Christy and Megan, her best friend. She came home the next day and we played volleyball outside and fixed lunch together. She was being extra nice to me. Late that night, the phone rang. It was too late for any of our friends to be calling. My mom answered and handed the phone to my sister. It was Megan.

Christy had been in a really bad car accident. They were in a navy blue sports car. It was Christy, her boyfriend, her best friend Andrea, and Andrea's boyfriend. The car flipped and got caught under a moving truck. None of them were wearing seat belts. Christy was thrown from the car. They found her ten feet from the accident. Andrea hit her head really hard on the dashboard. Andrea's boyfriend was thrown from the car and run over by the moving truck. He was under the front wheel when they found him. He died instantly. Christy's boyfriend only got a couple of scratches. The driver, Andrea's boyfriend was drunk. His blood alcohol level was .11. They said they didn't know he was drunk.

When Megan and my sister came back from the hospital, they said they couldn't even tell it was Christy. She had a broken hip bone, her tailbone was cracked, and her spine was damaged. The doctors said she would never be able to play sports again. She was more upset over this than anything. She loved softball, volleyball, and soccer.

I felt really sorry for her. I think everyone felt bad for her. She stayed in the hospital for about three and a half weeks. She stayed in bed for two weeks after leaving the hospital. She started going to therapy clinics not just to get her body to function right, but also for depression. She worked really hard that whole summer. At the end she was a lot better. Although she could hardly walk, she started going to the softball tournaments and cheering the team on. She didn't play that season, but the next summer she pitched and batted first. This shows that if you put your mind to something, you can achieve it, no matter what it is. Christy plays with my sister still today and is as healthy as ever.

LOSS OF A PET

Mittens

....

Destinee Leigh Downey, age 10

ON A WARM AND SUNNY AFTERNOON, MY PARENTS AND I went in search of a good family cat. We visited the animal shelter and I picked out more than three kittens. They were all diagnosed with a bad disease. I went into the little room where they kept the kittens. Looking at a fluffy gray kitten, I thought, "That cat is too skittish. She won't want to play with me."

My eyes then fell upon a black and white spotted kitten. He was adorable and had the cutest little beady eyes. His two paws were hanging out of the cage door. I took one look at the cat and said, "Mom, I want this one." We told the woman who worked there and she took some tests to see if he was healthy. To our luck, he had no diseases. We took him home in a cardboard kitty carrier. He purred and meowed when we took him out of the carrier to hold him. By the time we got home, he had fallen asleep. We put him on my bed and he awoke. Running about playfully, the little kitten seemed to have a personality similar to my own! The next day, the little creature was laying on me while I was asleep. I awoke and started playing with him, then he fell asleep.

As I watched him, I noticed something peculiar. He was sucking his front left paw. I quickly got my parents and they checked it out. We found out later that the kitten had been taken away from his mother too soon. I knew then that I would be his mother.

The next day, my mom and I were coming back from the store. I looked at the kitten and said, "I will name him Snowflake." I called him that name for a day or two, but it seemed too simple. A few days later, I was returning from my friend's house when I saw my kitten on the front porch step. "Hmm," I said, "that kitten deserves a name such as Loud Mouth." I named him that because he was always at the front porch step, meowing. But I thought that it was cruel to call him Loud Mouth, so my mom named him Mittens and I agreed. He had the shape of a little mitten on his forehead, and I thought it was a cute name. We stuck with that name.

Then, a month before we moved, Mittens disappeared. My mom thought he died. I knew that he found a better home. I had grown to love this cat and missed him dearly. We posted fliers around the area and even went to the Humane Society to look for him. We had moved five years earlier and we hadn't relicensed him. We ended up moving again, this time without him. I still have a little handkerchief that I used to put around his neck. It had paws printed on it. I miss him and still love him very much. Until this day, I know that he found a good home and he still thinks about me.

Molly

Elizabeth Patrick, age 9

I GOT A PUPPY. IT WAS A CUTE PUPPY. SHE WAS BLACK with a little white on her chest. I got her from my grandma and grandpa. She was a gift to me. She was very playful, joyful, and happy. When we had bonfires at night, she would jump up on the lawn chairs and sit. My grandma and I thought Molly thought she was a person. She may as well have been—she was my best friend in the world. She greeted me in the morning and again when I got back from school. When we came back from trips, she made sounds and jumped on us. She was the first dog I ever had. She will always be my favorite dog.

On October 28, Molly got hit by a car. Our neighbor called us and said there was black fur on the road. My dad went out to look, and there was Molly dead on the road. My parents didn't tell us until after school the next day. My dad came home early from work. He said he had something to tell us. We all came into the living room. He said that last night Molly got hit. When I heard that, I slammed a pillow down on the floor and hid my face in another one. I didn't believe it. I wanted to see her. My dad said she was out in the garage. We went to look, and there she saw.

"No, Molly! No, Molly!" I screamed. She was dead.

The next day I couldn't go to school because I thought I would cry. So Mom said I could stay home. She said, "You can't just sit around, though."

My mom's friend called on the phone and said she was sick. My mom asked if we could make dinner for them. She said, "yes." So we did. I peeled apples and potatoes. Then I made apple pie and apple sauce. Next I made brownies from scratch. The last thing I made was chocolate chip cookies. My mom made pizza potatoes out of the potatoes I peeled. Then we brought it over to them and they loved it.

Molly will always be my best friend. She was so special to me. I learned that if you help somebody when you feel sad, you make them feel good and you don't feel so sad anymore.

How I Saved a Dog's Life

....

Kate, age 7

WHEN MY OLD DOG, WINSTON, DIED, IT WAS SAD FOR ALL of us. So one day we went to the SPCA to look for a new dog. Of course, I knew we could never, ever, replace Winston, but if I didn't have a dog I would be sad forever. When I went in, I wanted every puppy in sight. Then I saw Shelly. I wanted her so badly, I thought my heart was going to hop right out of my chest. I had to get her.

Sometimes, the dogs at the SPCA are put to sleep if people don't buy them. Not this dog. I saved her.

Shelly is a very lucky puppy. She got a good owner, and she didn't have to be killed. I am glad she wasn't killed, and so is my whole family. Shelly is very cute and funny, but not always. Sometimes she gets into trouble. She is always cute, though.

To get her, we had to sign a sheet of paper, tell them what her name would be, and promise that we would take care of her. We had to promise to feed her the right food and to take her to the vet to get her shots.

I don't like to watch them give her shots, but I do anyway. I taught her some tricks, too. I taught her to catch the treat when I throw it in the air. And I taught her to fetch. I'm going to teach her more stuff, but I try to remember she is just a dog. Shelly is the best puppy in the world. I know that.

Sometimes I cry when I think of Winston. And sometimes Shelly makes me mad because she bites me. I don't like that. But I'm not the only one who gets bitten. My sister Katie, my mommy, and my step-dad also get bitten. She even bites herself sometimes. Other than that, she is a good puppy.

When I am grown up I'm going to be a veterinarian. I will help the sick puppies, especially Shelly. I really want to be a veterinarian. I hope I get the job because I like animals. And so does my friend. And I like God, too. And animals.

What I learned from my experience of getting a dog from the SPCA is that you need to give a dog a chance. You need to give them a good home to live in. And you need to treat them like any other person. You also need to give your love, and a lot of it.

You may cry sometimes when you remember your old dog. I do that a lot. I remember how I used to play with him. I bet other children will cry sooner or later if their dog dies, or maybe they already did. I'm glad to give them my experience for fair warning.

DEATH AND DYING

The Night
My Sister Died

....

Tyler Gregory Abrahamse, age 8

I HAD A BABY SISTER NAMED SADIE. SHE WAS BORN AFTER my birthday last January. She was very cute. I gave her the first bath in the hospital after she came out of my mom's stomach. My mom had her stomach cut open, so she was still sleeping and couldn't get out of bed to give Sadie a bath. I nicknamed my baby sister "Sweet Sadie" because she never cried. She let me hold her as she drank her bottle.

One night when she was seven weeks old, my mom was gone to a party, and my dad and brother and I were all watching a movie. We ate popcorn and stayed up late. When my brother and I went to bed, my dad went to pick up Sadie. She was sleeping in heaven.

I heard him scream. When I came upstairs, I saw a fireman come inside. My brother, Logan, was still sleeping and didn't hear a thing. I saw the fireman put down his box of stuff and start pushing on Sadie's stomach. My dad told me to go back to bed. I didn't know what happened. I saw many lights outside. I looked out my window through the blinds and saw my uncle's car.

When the ambulance man finally came, I figured out that my sister had died. It was very hard to see her lay there dead. My mom came home and my dad ran down the driveway to tell her. She screamed. She cried. She ran to me and hugged me so hard I cried. My aunt came and took me and my brother to my grandma's house.

It has been hard not having a sister anymore. I makes me sad. It makes my mom and dad sad, too. I try to think about what heaven is like, and what Sadie is doing there. I wonder if she is older than a baby in heaven. I want my mom to have another baby.

Sadie would be having her first birthday next week. I just had mine and it was fun. We went to the Rollerbarn and I had friends over. I helped make my cake and decorate it with soccer stuff on top. My mom even put soccer ball candles on it! I got lots of presents. We would have had a party and cake and presents for Sadie, too. I miss her.

My mom and dad sold our house and we are moving. I am glad. I am not going to school anymore, I'm staying home to do school. My mom and dad said I could. My teacher gave my mom all my books.

I like being home with my mom all day. She helps me feel better. She tells me she loves me and she is glad she has me. We do fun things together. I like to go hiking in the woods.

I miss my sister, but I know Sadie can never come back. I wish no babies ever got hurt or stopped breathing. I am glad there is heaven because she forgot to breathe. Someday, I want to be a doctor to fix people and babies so nobody dies. It makes everybody so sad.

This year without my sister has been the hardest time in my life. I hope next year is better. My mom and dad might take me to Disneyland. That would be fun. There is lots to do there, and I would like to see Mickey and Goofy.

The Gift of Time

Amanda Kowalski, age 12

A FEW YEARS AGO, MY GRANDMA DIED OF CANCER. SHE had both liver and bone cancer. I knew from the beginning that she would either be okay or she would die. Thinking about that was the hardest part, in the beginning. It was even harder when she came from each doctor's appointment with no sign of improvement. Since I knew that my grandma could die at almost any time, I visited her as often as I could. These visits with my grandma were very special.

It may not seem like it, but there was a miracle within this disaster, the miracle of time. She stayed alive with this often deadly disease for three years. It may seem like a lot, but it turned out to be just enough time for us to tell her how we truly felt.

I got a few more chances to tell my grandma that I loved her very much. We got the time to talk about the whole situation, and lots of other stuff, too. My family also appreciated the extra time with my grandma. In the beginning, the stress of everything tore the family apart. But over time, seeing her strength and courage made us realize that we needed to be there for her instead of fighting and arguing with each other.

One of the weekends we went to visit her, my mom said she was in pretty bad shape. She had said this many other times, so I didn't think much of it. When we got there, I went to see her. Even though she didn't look any worse, there was something different this time. The nurse that came to the house to check on her said that my grandma had only a few hours left.

It was then that I started to realize what my life would be like without my grandma. I started to remember all the good and bad times we had, and I tried to imagine what those last three years would have been like without having her there. It seemed far worse. That time with her truly was a miracle. Even with the bad luck of her getting cancer, how lucky we were to have had time.

That same day, my grandma died. Later that evening, an ambulance came and picked her up.

At the beginning of the next week, we went to a funeral home to get my grandma ready for the showing that was to take place later that afternoon. I had planned to say something, but I later decided not to. As I sat there at the showing, some of the songs and some of the things people said touched me. My uncle said, "She was a good person. In my heart, I believe she was taken from us, not because she was a bad person, but the exact opposite. She was too good a person. She was taken to heaven to be an angel. The change is not that she will be an angel, but that she will be an angel to all who need her, not just her family and friends." Those were and always will be my thoughts of her. She was an angel in my life, and now she'll be an angel in many people's lives.

After the showing, the funeral was planned for exactly one week later. It would be held in her home town in Alabama. The funeral was not as hard as the showing was. We sang "Amazing Grace" and I took home a flower. We went back to my great-grandpa's house and had a big lunch. We were all sad, of course, but we managed to have a good time during and after lunch. We all knew that Grandma was in a place where she didn't have to suffer anymore. I think this made us all feel a little better.

After I returned home, I began to miss her a lot. Any and all spare time was spent thinking about everything she taught me and remembering all the times I spent with her. Good or bad, the thought of being with her was reassuring. Every memory brought a tear, and every tear brought a whole new memory. It was like my whole life with my grandma was being recycled. I knew that sooner or later, when the cycle stopped, I would feel better. Of course, the cycle wouldn't just stop, it would take my whole life for the memories and tears and pain to wear too thin to remember.

I would much rather this not have happened, but since it has, I am slowly learning to deal with it.

When It Rains, It Pours

....

Cheryl Ann, age 12

IT ALL STARTED ONE NOVEMBER NIGHT IN 1996. MOM had just gotten off the phone with her sister, my Aunt Vicki. She didn't look so good. She had been crying. She called to all of us to come sit on her bed. I could tell something was wrong. The first thing I thought was that someone had died.

Mom sat there trying not to cry, then slowly said, "Uncle Perry has cancer, terminal cancer." The room was completely silent. We sat there stunned. Then, I started to cry. My brother and sister really hadn't gotten to know our uncle. I knew him only slightly. My best friend in the world is his daughter, my cousin Carla. Months earlier I had spent two weeks at their dairy in Washington, and she spent two weeks with us in the city. I love her so much and I couldn't imagine how much pain she was going through. I was crying for her.

Mom and Dad had decided to go on a cruise in March. Our aunt and uncle were going on one in February. They decided to go on the same ship, the one in February. During the beginning of February our uncle died from cardiac arrest before the painful part of the cancer had begun.

That morning, Mom gathered us around the couch and told us the terrible news. That day, we each bought a balloon, drove to the nearest dairy farm, and let them go as the cows were gathering around us.

Aunt Vicki got a refund, but Mom and Dad couldn't, so they still went on the cruise in February. That week was one of the hardest weeks of my young life. My dad's parents took care of us and I got a small taste of what it would be like without my parents. It gave me time to think about stuff. Perry was only forty-two years old and had four kids. Dad is forty-one and has three kids. It hit me so hard, how fast a loved one could die.

Mom and Dad returned from their cruise to some problems too personal to reveal in this essay. But our family was strong enough to work these through. Little did we know what would come.

My brother was diagnosed at a young age with ADD (Attention Deficit Disorder). He never really was a social kid. As he got older he started having some difficulties. He attempted suicide twice. He always did get along better with Mom that he did with Dad. That really bothered my dad. One day, Dad asked him to put on his shoes so we could go into a restaurant. Mom wasn't there, and my brother refused to take orders from Dad. He got violent and Dad started to drive him to the hospital. Going down a road at 35 to 40 miles an hour, he opened the car door and attempted to jump out. That was extremely frightening for my sister and me. My brother saw a doctor, who diagnosed him with bipolar disorder.

We went on with our lives, as hard as that was, but eventually we admitted him to the hospital. It was awful. For seven days he was heavily medicated, even to the level where the medicine became toxic to his body. When Mom realized what was going on, she moved him to a different hospital. At the new place, they noticed that his tongue was swelling. He was having a toxic reaction from the drugs. They gave him a shot and he was okay. When the new doctor saw him, he recognized that my brother had Asperger syndrome, a form of autism. The diagnosis seems to fit and he likes his new doctor. He has been consistently getting better. It's great to have him back.

As I struggled through these hard times, I constantly called Carla in Washington. She always listened and had a caring word to share. Just knowing she was there to listen when I needed to talk gave me the courage to continue. We were there for each other.

I've learned a great deal from my experiences. I've learned to treasure every moment you spend with your loved ones. I've learned to love everyone as they are and that I can't expect someone to change. I've learned that no matter how alone you feel, there's always someone who will listen, and talking always helps. Knowing someone is there when you need them really helps. I hope other kids don't have to go through what I did, but we all have hard times in one form or another. After all, it is the difficult times in life that strengthen us and develop our character. It may not be any fun to go through the trials, but if we face them instead of run away, we grow. Remember, after every storm is a beautiful rainbow. But it appears *after* the rain.

The Night of Sorrow

Maren, age 12

It was early morning on March 27, 1991. My mom and sister, Marissa, were sitting next to my bed, sobbing. I was in bewilderment, so I asked what was the matter. They looked at each other and then back at me. My mom reached out to hold my hand as she said, "Honey, we have bad news. Daddy died in a car accident last night."

I was shocked. I asked if they were serious. They nodded their heads. There was a long silence in the room. We all just sat there hugging each other and crying. I couldn't believe what they were telling me.

Later on, I found out what had happened. My sister worked at Dairy Queen. She couldn't drive yet, so my dad went to pick her up. It was late and the roads were slippery. As my father entered a tunnel, he swerved and hit a safety bar, which threw him into the back seat. He was wearing his seat belt, but the force was too strong. The police officer told my mom that in the last two seconds of his life he probably thought about two things: his wife and his children. All of this happened while Marissa waited for her ride home. There are still some mysteries of this accident I'll probably never come to know for sure.

Over the seven years since the accident, I have overcome that horrible night. I think I have survived this tragedy well, and so have my mom and sister, whom I love very much. There are many things that have helped me recover. I went to counseling for a long time and I belonged to a grief support group called Evergreen. My family also shares stories about our relationships with my dad. To help the healing, when it's my dad's birthday, we usually go to the cemetery and lay flowers next to his grave. We let balloons float up into the sky and we watch them until they disappear. We do this at Christmas and also on the anniversary of his death.

When my dad was alive, he loved to travel. My father was a construction manager and flew around the country building stores. We enjoyed going on family trips, too. We visited many places together, like Florida, New England, Pennsylvania, the East Coast, and all over Ohio. Marissa, Mom, and I have continued to travel together since his death. We feel he is traveling with us.

My dad had many hobbies. He enjoyed singing, playing the guitar, fishing, cooking, going to concerts, and laughing and joking with his family. He loved nature and watching sports on TV, especially football. He was a Miami Dolphins fan as well as an Ohio Buckeyes fan.

I miss Dad a lot. I miss the things I did with him and the things he did for me. When I was little, he took me fishing at Hoover Dam because I had one chicken pock and had to miss school. We caught a couple of fish and brought them home to eat. My dad helped me play the piano because he loved music. He was very supportive of me when I took jazz lessons, and he always came to my recitals. He would take all of us to King's Island and would spin us on the teacups until we would laugh and get dizzy. He was a wonderful dad, and people always comment on how much I look like him.

From the experience of losing my dad when I was only six, I learned that things can happen unexpectedly at any time. Sometimes these things can really tear your world apart. It takes a lot of strength for my mom to support Marissa and me on her own. One really important thing is that my family is very close. We share our feelings and encourage each other every day.

When a tragedy like this happens to kids, it is important to get help and talk about it with people you can trust. What my family and I have learned from this night of sorrow is that life can be short, so make every day count. I very much understand kids who have lost a loved one at a young age, because I've been there.

ILLNESS AND DISABILITY

Believing in Myself

....

Joshua Jay L., age 10

HI. MY NAME IS JOSHUA AND I'M TEN YEARS OLD. I'M IN the fourth grade. I seemed to have problems in school pronouncing words, understanding what I read, talking loud enough, and even doing some math problems. This led to me being put in corrective reading and math classes. There seemed to be a slight improvement, but I still needed more help.

The next step was to be tested by the school psychologist. I was diagnosed with learning disabilities. The school psychologist told my mom and dad that I had trouble grasping every word the teacher said. I needed help with my vowel sounds, speaking out in class, and other skills. The psychologist did say that I had potential and, with some hard work, could improve. They decided to keep me in the corrective classes but added speech class to the list.

I was upset. It was bad enough that I was in two of those classes, now they had added another one. I was angry at myself. I felt different from the other kids. I had no confidence in myself. I was afraid to speak in front of others because I felt they would laugh at me if I pronounced a word wrong. So I began writing my thoughts and feelings on paper. Then one day my mom saw an article in one of her magazines about a club for kids who like to write.

I joined the club, called The Write News. Every month or so, they have a contest in their newsletter. I decided to enter one of my essays and, to my surprise, I won! After that, I won about three or four other times. I also won a contest in school for a poem I wrote.

This made me believe in myself. I'm working harder at school and starting to read a lot better in class. I'm no longer afraid to speak in front of my classmates.

I'm still in corrective classes, but my teachers have seen a great improvement in me. They are great. With their help and the help of my family, I found the strength to overcome my disabilities.

I hope my story will help other children with learning disabilities to overcome their fears and to believe in themselves. I hope each of them will become the confident person that I have become.

My Hero

....

Kari Jo Johnson, age 10

LET ME START AT THE BEGINNING. ZACHARY WAS BORN on May 21, 1991. It was a great thing in my life until we found out he had Down's syndrome. My story is about going through the stress of having a family member born with a disability.

My parents and I sat down and talked about what was wrong with Zach and how it was going to affect our lives. Mom said it was going to be a struggle, but with a lot of love and encouragement, we could help Zach live a happy life.

Zach wasn't very old when we found out about another problem. My parents and I sat down again, this time to talk about cancer. Zach had leukemia. I felt like my whole life was being ruined. I felt bad because I knew we would have to go through yet another struggle, and this time we might lose Zach.

It was really hard. I barely got to see my parents because they were always at the hospital with Zach. I knew that Zach was doing well at the hospital. Mom and Dad had confidence in the doctors, and we had lots of prayers and support to get us through.

One time, when I was in third grade, we were watching a movie about children with cancer. During the movie, somebody made fun of a kid who had cancer. I leaned over to my friend and said, "If that ever happened to Zach, I would say, 'It is not his fault that he has cancer.'" My friend leaned over and told me, "If that ever happened and you weren't there, I would tell them that, too." I almost cried.

Zach has been cancer-free for five years now, but living with Down's syndrome isn't easy. My mom always tells me what a good sister I am. Every day, with my help, Zach gets on the bus and goes to school. He is in first grade and is doing very well. I help him try to talk, say his ABCs, and count to ten.

Zach tries really hard to do the things that other kids his age do. Some things are easier than others, but most of the time he struggles. Zach doesn't really know that he has a handicap, he just enjoys his many books, his many, many movies, and, most of all, his family. I think our family has become closer and more special because of Zach's disability and his cancer.

I once had a dream—and I still do—that Zach would be treated as a normal person. Someday I know he will be a person that other kids look up to. I wish that someday Zach will be known all around Minnesota for being a person who came out on top.

It all started when Zach was born and I thought my life was ruined. Now, I wouldn't trade my life or my family for anything in the world. He is my hero, and I love him very much.

Something Deadly

Galen Halbart, age 11

A POPCORN KERNEL, SOMETHING DEADLY. A POPCORN kernel that ruined my sister's life at age fourteen months. A popcorn kernel. Disaster.

Suddenly, Sarah started choking. My dad quickly slapped her on the back to get the stuck object out of her throat. The coughing stopped. A popcorn kernel slipped lower into my sister's lung. Late, late that night, she started coughing. My mom and dad were worried so they let her sleep in their bed with them.

Early in the morning, she stopped breathing. My mom rushed to the phone to call 911. Because of the noise, I woke up when the paramedics were working on her. I went down the steps to see what all the racket was about. I found them putting Sarah in an ambulance. The CPR they tried had not worked.

My dad's cousin, one of the paramedics who showed up at our house, stayed with me and my older sister. Mom and Dad went to the hospital to be with Sarah. Her heart was stopped for twenty-five minutes. She would have been a goner, but technology saved her life. She did not, however, survive without critical damage to her brain. She was in a coma for six weeks and the brain damage resulted in cerebral palsy. This means she cannot move her muscles the way she wants them to move.

There are a lot of difficulties that result from Sarah's disability. One of them is that Sarah needs constant attention because she can't take care of herself. Personal care attendants help us take care of Sarah, and we couldn't do it without them. But sometimes they show up late or not at all, and sometimes they're hard to find. At times, they are more bother than they are worth.

Another difficulty is the limited amount of handicap-accessible houses and buildings. Most have too many stairs to bring her wheelchair up and down. Some places don't have enough parking spaces, and a lot of places don't have any ramps. In addition, many sidewalks, pathways, and trails are unsuitable for wheelchairs. We also are limited in where we can go for vacation, because cabins and campgrounds are not very accessible.

One way to cope with a disability is to use special devices—special computer programs, lifts, communication devices, push buttons, special switches, and so on—but these all come with their own problems. The biggest is cost. Although these devices are useful, they cannot be made in mass quantities. The result: they cost a lot more than similar items made for people without disabilities. They are also hard to find.

Life has changed tremendously for my whole family. We all spend a lot of time with Sarah. She needs constant attention. Everyone chips in a chunk of their time to help her. I can't explain everything that her disability has changed in my life, because I don't know life without her having a disability. Sarah's disability has not only caused tremendous change for my family, it has also caused tremendous pain. It's like carrying a burden too heavy to hold. All I can say is that it isn't fair.

We have adapted our lives to help make things easier for Sarah. For example, we moved to a one-level house and built a ramp for her wheelchair. We also remodeled our bathroom so she could get in with her wheelchair.

Even though the disability is not reversible, my family has done much to help Sarah get through her life. For example, the governor was going to cut the Children's Home Care Option and PCA benefits. I helped by going to the capitol with my friends, my mom, and my sister to protest against the cuts. It worked, because they didn't make the cuts.

We do not want Sarah to have to go through a lot of medical procedures, although she had to get a gastrostomy tube, a way to get food directly into her stomach, because she could not eat. We also have tried some things to loosen her muscles.

Sarah enjoys life. She is very popular. Almost everyone knows her. She also has a couple of close friends who come to our house to play with her. She takes dance with other kids in wheelchairs. Dance class is one of her favorite activities. In dance class, they dance to music from Disney movies and musicals. They even do the Macarena and some polkas. Some of the kids, like Sarah, who cannot move their arms and legs without help, have people to assist them. You can just see how thrilled they are to be dancing—their whole body smiles.

Sarah is a neat and interesting person. Her disability has helped me understand a lot about life. If it weren't for her, I don't think I would have as much knowledge. But still, my biggest wish would be for her to recover, even though that would be impossible. She's one of the only people I know who can outshine the sun.

My Brother

....

Chelsea L.H., age 9

MY BROTHER, COREY, IS DIFFERENT FROM ME. NO, IT IS not because he is a boy, or because he is older than I am. It is because he is handicapped.

Corey can't do things other people can do. He can't talk right and has trouble learning things. He goes to a special school for handicapped kids. They help him learn how to talk. He has learned how to go up to the counter at a fast-food place and order his own food, and more.

It is harder to have a handicapped brother than a non-handicapped brother, because it's hard to go places. He gets afraid when we go out to eat or go shopping because he thinks he is going to the doctor or the dentist. It makes him become physical. We can't go anywhere when Corey is home.

One of the things I have learned by living with a handicapped brother is that I can love other people, even if they are different from me. I have learned to be patient. It takes Corey longer to get dressed, and it is harder for him to learn things. I have also become a good helper because of Corey. I have to help Mom and Dad with Corey because they are tired from working all day. I often help Corey get dressed and get a shower. I have learned to have a sense of humor because of Corey. He makes me laugh when he does funny things. He loves me a lot. Sometimes he picks me up and twirls me around. He even dances with me.

Other kids might learn a lot by having a handicapped brother. It could teach them not to laugh at other people who are different. I now know not to laugh or stare at older people or people in wheelchairs. Other children need to learn not to laugh when they hear handicapped people talk. They need to really listen and try to understand what is being said. Other kids might want to be patient like I am, because not everyone learns as fast as others.

I believe we are fortunate that God put us on this earth so we can be with each other. We need to learn to accept each other just the way we are. A lot of my friends I have met these past years in school have thought Corey is weird. I say he is special. I love my brother, just the way he is.

I'm Starting to Like Life

....

A.J., age 12

I HAVE DONE SO MANY DIFFERENT THINGS IN MY LIFE, I don't know where to begin. I think I'll begin by introducing myself.

My name is A.J. and I'm twelve. I am 5'1", which has advantages and disadvantages. I'm taller than most of my friends, but shorter than my brother. I have brown hair and brown eyes. I live with my dad, mom, brother, sister, and our dog. Having an older brother and a younger sister is sometimes fun and sometimes not.

Life for me wasn't always happy. I was born with a nevus, or birthmark, that covered my entire back. The doctor said I had to have it removed before I got cancer. At the hospital, the surgeon performed five operations on me before I was three, and then two more when I was eight and nine.

I was sad and angry after my operations. I was even so mad that I didn't want to walk anymore. I don't know if I did that because of the pain or my anger. The stitches that were on my back hurt badly, but I know I'll be all right now. I learned that even though having surgery can be scary, it can really help you.

When I was in fourth grade, my friend and I went up to his uncle's cabin and we gathered maple syrup. We also went snowboarding, played games, playing in the snow, and went on tractor rides. Meeting some of my friend's cousins was fun because we could play lots of games, such as Tag, Hide-and-Go-Seek, and War. Gathering maple syrup and having fun was great. I hope I can go up there again. I enjoy the wilderness.

Every year, my family and I go up to my grandparents' cabin. Renting a pontoon, driving around for the day, and eating lunch on the pontoon is something we do every year since we started. Just last year, Papa and Grammy made a bunk house just for us kids. Helping my dad and Papa around the cabin is fun. Last year I helped set up the flagpole. This year we are planning to repaint most of the cabin.

Without my surgery, I might not have been able to do all the things that I told you about. Life is full of surprises; I'm glad I'll be around to discover them.

A Walk through the Valley of the Shadow of Death

....

Amanda Moore, age 10

WHEN I WAS FIVE, I WAS DIAGNOSED WITH LEUKEMIA, A type of cancer marked by the loss of white blood cells. It started with unexplained aches and pains. Within a week, I could no longer walk. I was sent to my local hospital where, for the next five days, I went through many painful tests. My doctor then sent me to Miami Children's Hospital, where I was diagnosed with leukemia. In one moment, life as I knew it was no longer the same.

For the next seven months, the hospital became my second home. All around me were strange faces and terrifying procedures, such as spinal taps and bone marrow exams. Life in the hospital was interesting, though. Privacy was limited. A lot of times, I found myself in one room with two other patients and their parents! It was noisy and hectic with only a curtain separating us. The food was nasty. A lot of people spoke Spanish, which made the hospital confusing at times.

For kindergarten and half of my first-grade year, I had to be taught at home by a teacher because I might have caught an illness from a classmate. When I finally was allowed to go to school, I was unable to participate in PhysEd. This was because of a mediport transplanted into my chest that couldn't be dislodged or I could bleed to death. The mediport was where medicine was injected over and over again. I also was unable to eat in the lunchroom because of all the germs.

Chemotherapy lasted over three years. I still have occasional blood tests done. I will be watched closely until I am twenty-one. I am almost eleven now. When I am thirteen, I will be considered officially cured.

My family is made up of a father, mother, two brothers, and a sister. I find a lot of comfort in them. My faith in God and His Word helps me to face each and every day. It is easy to comfort others in pain because I understand how they feel. I have shared my experiences with large groups of people and have not found it difficult. I have been interviewed many times for many different events. I have made speeches for the American Cancer Society, and the Make-a-Wish Foundation granted me a wish: to go to North Carolina to see my relatives and go to a Nascar race. I was treated like royalty the whole week. I also had a chance to go to a cancer camp twice. It helped to be in camp with other people who have the same illness as I do. One of my favorite experiences was when I went 120 miles an hour in a pace car, with a real Indy car driver!

I enjoyed returning to my old life. God helped me overcome my illness by giving me strength to go on with my life. Now that I'm off chemotherapy, my family and I enjoy traveling. Our two favorite destinations are Asheville, North Carolina, and the Florida Keys. For almost a year, I have been taking English riding lessons. I like going to school and feel sorry for kids who can't. It's been great having so many relatives to see me through hard times. Many people have run in my honor to raise money for cancer research. Dr. Gowda, my local doctor, was very special to me because when I was sad, he would make me happy. Having gone through the valley of the shadow of death, I realize that every breath is a gift from God.

Living with ADD

....

C.M.S., age 9

MY STORY IS ABOUT LIVING WITH ATTENTION DEFICIT Disorder (ADD) and always feeling left out. You may think you know what hard is, but you don't. You don't know what it feels like to be left out, to always know you don't fit in.

For as long as I can remember, I haven't fit in. I feel like I don't fit with my family. The conversations never include me. I'm constantly being told to be quiet, stop laughing, or stop jumping. Sometimes I feel like I'm being told to stop being me. That's basically the present, so now I'll tell you about the past.

I didn't start to have problems until first grade. My mom says that's normal. I guess it's because kindergarten is mostly playing, so it's easy to pay attention. Anyway, in first grade, when I "stared into space," my teacher slapped my hand or hit my desk. I paid attention, but I started to stare into space again. I guess I can't blame her, though; she didn't know.

In second grade, I had the most wonderful teacher. She knew I was smart and that it wasn't my fault I couldn't pay attention. She was the first to think I might have a learning problem. I went to the school psychologist. He thought so, too.

Third grade was pure torture. My teacher always yelled and was always comparing me to my cousin, her pet, Little Miss Perfect. One time she said to me, "If you don't get your act together, you are going to fail."

Last summer I went to a doctor who did some tests. It turned out that I have ADD, but the good news is that there are medicines to help. The doctor put me on Ritalin. At first it was really hard for me to accept. One night when I was at my grandma's house, I started crying because I felt like I wasn't normal, and I just couldn't stop. I guess I was crying about everything that had ever happened to me.

Now I am in fourth grade and I have two great teachers. I pay attention and finish my work now. So far, I have had a great year. I love to read, and my teachers say that I'm a good writer. When I grow up I want to be a university English literature professor.

Living with ADD has been a challenge, but I'm doing better. My mom says that God won't give you challenges you can't handle. I learned a lot of things, but the two most important things I learned are to never give up and never judge a person right away. If everyone were to give up every time something becomes hard, nothing would ever get done. If George Washington had given up, we would still be part of England. A lot of the world's problems are caused by people judging other people too quickly. Slavery was caused by white people thinking they were better than everyone else. That's my story, and being able to share it makes me feel really good.

Twelve-Year-Old
with a Broken Leg

....

Marcus Fitzgerald, age 12

IT WAS A GLOOMY WEDNESDAY NIGHT IN OCTOBER. I had a football game at Bottineau Park at 7:30 P.M. Before the game I was thinking about how I would play. I had a feeling we were going to kill the Boosters. Their record was 0 and 8.

It began to rain just as the game started. I didn't get to go in for the kick return, but the halfback, Jason, returned the kick for ten yards. The next play, we ran the ball to the left of the center, and then we scored a touchdown! A sixty-yard run by Jason. Our fans went crazy. We were screaming and hollering, and we scored the extra point.

It was our turn to kick off. The ref blew his whistle and our kicker, Jeff, kicked the ball. I ran down the field as fast as I could. A player from the other team was running with the ball right toward me. I was going to knock his lights out. Then it happened: I was coming up to make the hit when all of a sudden, the player slipped and flew in the air horizontally. He came down on my leg.

The next moment I tried to get up, but my leg from my knee down was bent 40 degrees to the left.

I didn't feel any pain. I tried to calm down and just laid there while people came out to help. Jason's mom is a nurse. Thank God she was there, because nobody else knew what they were doing.

When the ambulance came, the medical technicians asked the coach what had happened. They wanted to give me a shot before they tried to get me in the ambulance. I thought I would never walk again. When they gave me the shot, I turned my head the other way. I prayed that it wouldn't hurt and that everything would get better. As they put me in the ambulance, the whole team crowded around me. I told them, "Don't give up," and I said to Jason, "Do a power sweep."

On the way to the hospital, I turned to my mom and said, "Mom, I took the pain like a man. I didn't cry or scream." She smiled and said, "Right on, Marcus."

Ten minutes later we arrived at the hospital. I was put in a room to watch TV and wait. My dad and brother came to look at my leg. They looked shocked and sad. After about thirty minutes, I was about to go into surgery. Dr. Olson told me he was going to put a pin the size of a knitting needle all the way through my leg and put two screws in my leg to cover the growth plate.

As he wheeled me into the operating room, I looked at all the things in that room. I wondered what they would do to me. They put a mask over my face so they could put me to sleep.

Eight hours later, I woke up in a room with my mom. I looked down to see the cast on my leg. How was I going to get around with that big cast? At 2:30, friends from school came to see me. They brought me a lollipop, a Beanie Baby, and card. My dad came to see me, and then he and my mom had to leave. Other family, friends, and teachers dropped by, each bearing gifts to cheer me up.

When I went home, the first thing I did was sit in the Lazyboy chair and relax. But the worst part was that I had to urinate in a little cup. I just hated it. Whenever I urinated, someone would have to take it, pour it in the toilet, and rinse it out.

That night, nothing could get me to sleep. I tossed and I turned. At 4:30 A.M., I was still awake. My leg was killing me.

Two weeks later it was time to get the big cast off and get a hard cast. When I got to the doctor's office, a woman cut off my cast. I thought there'd be a lot of cuts on my leg from the surgery, but when she took the cast off, there were only two scabs on the inside of my right leg and a big pin sticking out with scabs around it. The woman brought out fiberglass for the hard cast and Dr. Olson wrapped it around my leg. Ten minutes later, the cast was getting very cold because fiberglass gets cold when it hardens.

The next week, I went back to school. My classmates all signed my cast. My friend Mike, who sits in the desk behind me, really helped me a lot. He helped me with anything I needed. When I went back to the doctor to take off the cast, the bone was not completely mended back together. When the cast was cut off, it looked nastier than when I saw it the first time. There were lots of scabs on the right and left of my leg. Dr. Olson took some x-rays of my knee and said I was healing fast. When they pulled the pin out of my leg, I closed my eyes and held my mom's hand. I prayed it wouldn't hurt when, Wap! The pin was out of my leg.

I wore a big brace for the next two weeks and still had to use crutches. When those weeks were over, I felt like a new man! Now I am back in sports and will probably play football next year. I had been playing football for four years and I wasn't going to stop.

God really gave me a wake-up call. I know that the boy who slid into my leg didn't mean to hurt me. The next time I go on the field, I won't intend to hurt somebody.

I pray that nobody else gets hurt like I did. Having a broken leg taught me that you need people to help you. I also learned that people with physical disabilities need to be loved, cared for, and treated with sensitivity and respect. After one week of feeling sorry for myself, I realized how grateful I was to have supportive friends, family, and doctors who helped me before I went into surgery.

What other kids can learn from my story is that you can recover and that you should never give up. The battle seems hard at first, but you just have to keep going because life doesn't stop. Just because I broke my strongest leg doesn't mean that I will stop playing football. And remember to put your trust in God and let Him take over.

FAMILY

My Parents' Divorce

....

Austin, age 12

MY NAME IS AUSTIN AND I AM TWELVE YEARS OLD. MY parents got a divorce because they are two different people. My mom likes computers and my dad likes horses. When they separated, it was very, very hard on me and my brother.

When they told us, it was like someone ripped my heart out, tore it in two, and put half back in. My brother's heart shattered like thin glass. I got over that part, but you don't know how hard it was. I almost never forgave them for doing that to us.

My dad is always working, and the agreement was that he would get us every weekend. Sometimes I see him every four weekends. One time he was going to pick us up, but he didn't and I was heartbroken. He has done that many times, but it does not bother me anymore.

My mom has a boyfriend now, and he is so much fun. He wrestles with us and plays with us all the time. Sometimes we spend the night over at his house on Fridays. But he does not live in the best neighborhood. Sometimes in the middle of the summer we go to his house. There are three pools in his neighborhood and it is fun.

My dad has got a new girlfriend, too, and she has a daughter. I was very stupid and liked her. We became girlfriend and boyfriend, but after our vacation we became enemies. My dad is treating her better than he treats his own sons. I think she and her mother are witches and have a spell on my dad. I don't see what my dad sees in her. The only things I see are ugliness and meanness. When I try to act like a gentleman to her, she just gives me a dirty look.

I am getting over it . . . by ignoring it.

Is Your Mom Having a Baby?

Derek William Jannarone, age 9

I KNOW WHAT YOU MUST FEEL LIKE IF YOUR MOTHER IS pregnant. You probably feel that everyone will "ooh" and "aah" over the baby and you'll get less and less attention. I know when my mom was pregnant I was scared. I didn't know what to do. I was happy about it, but at the same time I didn't know how everything would change for me.

I had two older sisters and a brother, but they were in college, so I was the only one in the house. I felt like an only child. My mother was cranky sometimes, but I found that if I just listened she was all right.

It was when I went to kindergarten that my sister was born. I remember that after she was born I took the day off from school to go see her.

My grandparents came all the way from Arkansas to see her. I was happy about being a big brother and my parents were excited, too. To my surprise, my grandparents still paid a lot of attention to me. And, when we had other company, I remember getting lots of attention after they met my little sister, so everything was fine.

When my sister, Sarah, started to crawl, we had to put baby locks on all the cabinets and couldn't have anything lying around. That was a pain, but I looked forward to her getting older so I would have someone to play with. Plus, when you're older, you can get paid for baby-sitting!

For about a year, we had a lot of company who always seemed to be saying, "Look how big she is!" and "She's so cute!" It wasn't always easy, but it turned out all right.

My sister is now four, and I am nine. She helps me with my chores and we get along great. So, if your mom is going to have a baby and you're worried about how it'll change things for you, just relax. Don't be scared. It's like all new things—it just takes a little time to get used to.

Adoption Can Be Hard

....

TAH, age 12

HELLO. MY NAME IS TINA. I LIVE IN MINNESOTA, AND I'm twelve years old. I'm in sixth grade.

When I was about three, I moved to a foster home where there were five members in the family. When I was staying there, they adopted a wonderful African girl. That made me very sad because they didn't adopt me. The family was nice to me. Like most people, we had our ups and downs once in a while, but not often.

When I was seven, I went to a counseling center. There was a very kind man who chauffeured me to and from counseling. He was not only my chauffeur, but my friend as well. And when I was at counseling, a black-haired woman would talk to me. I didn't really want to talk about my problems at first, but after a while I started to like talking about things. She really helped me. There were days I felt like I would never have a real family, but she made me feel better. She made me feel like there was hope.

I went to counseling every other day. After counseling, my chauffeur would come pick me up. Sometimes we would go out for dinner or to the Dairy Queen for a treat, and sometimes we would just go home.

When I was nine, the best thing happened to me. I was adopted. At my adoption, my biological mom didn't show up, so I can't see her until I'm eighteen. After I thought about it for a while, I realized that she wouldn't see me graduate. Right now, school is the most important thing to me. I know my real parents love me and I love them.

When I was adopted, I had to change schools. That was really hard, until I met Julie. She is the greatest friend anyone could ever have. She showed me around the school and helped me make friends. After the first week of school, I wasn't known as "the new girl." I'm in sixth grade now and everything is going fine. I have nice teachers and a principal who used to be my teacher.

If you have the same problem I had, talk to someone. It makes a difference. You don't deserve to suffer for someone else's mistake. Talk it out. When you are hurt inside, you're not a very kind person on the outside or the inside. So please talk to someone.

SELF-ESTEEM

Shy

Molly Brooks, age 9

WHEN I WAS LITTLE, I WAS SHY. I'LL PROBABLY ALWAYS BE shy, but I'm not as shy as I used to be.

My mom loved to travel. We went to Europe when I was eighteen months old. I had a friend who didn't speak my language. She spoke German. We talked but couldn't understand each other. Only, we did play. When I was two and a half, we moved to Africa. I made friends there. They spoke Lingala. I started to pick up on it, but we had to move because there was a war. That was when I was three. We moved back to California, and then, when I was four, we moved to Denver. I guess living in so many different places with different cultures and new people made me afraid to meet new people.

When I was in preschool, I never played with anyone except a girl named Christina. I am still friends with her, even though we go to different elementary schools. She is one of my best friends.

On Halloween, I was afraid to show my Jasmine costume from the movie *Aladdin,* which my mom made. I wouldn't go to my preschool Halloween party. I cried at the Halloween party at church.

When I was in kindergarten, I was very shy. When I knew an answer I wouldn't raise my hand because I was too afraid to talk to the teacher. Soon I got to know my teacher better and wasn't as shy with her. But I was very shy with the kids in my class. At recess I never played with anyone. One day my teacher asked a girl named Mirth to play with me. I played with her and her friends but never talked to them.

A girl from Florida came to our school. Her name was Robin. I started playing with her. She was very nice. I even went over to her house. She lives in her uncle's basement. My mom met her mom and they became friends. The house across the street from our house was for sale. It was an attractive yellow house, and my mom persuaded them to get it. After that, Robin and I were always playing.

Soon kindergarten was over. Robin and I were in the same first-grade class. Our teacher's name was Mrs. Bleau. I had many friends in the first grade. I have to say I was pretty popular. First grade was one of my most favorite grades. I did very well in school. I read *James and the Giant Peach* and was the star in a play called *War on the Home Front.* Everyone wanted me to be the star because the star's name was Molly, just like me. My mom was worried about me, but I did really well.

I wasn't in Robin's class in second grade, but I made lots of new friends. I was in classes for gifted and talented kids at school, and I was kind of quiet. I did make two friends, though, Jessica and Laurie. We played with Beanie Babies and sometimes we played Monkeys and Tag. Let's just say we played a lot of different games. My mom did Art Start in my class, which was really fun. It was pretty neat. I had a part in the second-grade musical. I didn't sing, I just said one line. Second grade was really fun. I liked my class very much.

In third grade we had to do an animal report. By this time, I wasn't shy at all. I am in a program called Odyssey of the Mind. We did a play and I worked in a catering truck. We get to go to state finals. I am still in third grade and just did a report on Clara Barton. I dressed up like her for six different classes. Everyone liked my report.

With the help of my family and friends, I am not as shy as I used to be. I have learned that it is okay to be shy, but it is more fun not to be. If I remember that it is okay to be shy, then I am sure I will have a great life. I also learned that being shy is like being embarrassed, and I don't have to be embarrassed for anything. Other people can learn from this. Everyone should just be himself or herself, and so should I.

A Difficult Time

....

John B. Giorgilli, III, age 11

A DIFFICULT TIME IN MY LIFE WAS JUST GOING THROUGH
fifth grade. To give you some background, we had just
moved from Baltimore to Millville, otherwise known as
"lower, slower Delaware." I transferred from a school that
I had gone to my whole life and enrolled in the local elementary school, which I would only stay in for one year.
After fifth grade, I would again move to another school,
Selbeyville Middle School. This would represent three different schools in three years.

During fifth grade, I didn't make many friends. I was
different. The other students picked on me because of the
way I looked (I have red hair and freckles) and because I
didn't have the money to go out and buy a $45 shirt or $50
shoes. They also picked on me because I didn't have the
money to buy the best of the best sports equipment.
However, they mostly picked on me because they thought
I was weird and awkward. The kids at school never picked
me for their team, and they treated me like I was invisible
to them. Their actions, as well as lack of interaction, made
me feel bad about myself.

I have been a student of martial arts, specifically Tae Kwon Do, since I was eight. The boys in fifth grade made fun of this sport because they didn't understand how to do it or what it means. When they chose to pick on this sport, it made me feel even worse about myself, because it is the only thing I am really good at. Tae Kwon Do is the study of discipline, self-esteem, and self-confidence. Martial arts training has done wonders for me as a person, sibling, and student.

My parents and teachers tried to help, but all I did was push them away. I told them I didn't need their help, although I really did. I never would admit that I needed help because I didn't want them to think I couldn't deal with my own problems. I finally gave in and talked to them about what was bothering me.

After my parents, teachers, and school counselor helped me learn to deal with these kids, I was a new me. The counselor helped with my emotions, too, by teaching me different ways to deal with my anger and lack of self-worth. Now I know that the key to a good life is what is on the inside, not what is on the outside. You must accept that some people are just down-right mean and do not want to be an "uncool" person's friend, and you must not let that keep you from going on.

I did make one friend—Gretchen. She was the only person to become my friend almost the whole year. Gretchen is the fairest and kindest girl I will ever know. She befriended me when no one else would, and this helped me tremendously. We are still very good friends.

I overcame this difficult situation with the help of a friend, my teachers, my family, and the school counselor. They helped me by telling me that it is okay to be different and that I am fine just the way I am. That is how I made my way through fifth grade.

I am now a sixth grader in a new school with many friends. I know that just being me is fine. I take the time to stand up for kids my own age who need help like I did. I have learned to accept myself for who I am. This was difficult at first because of the poor self-image I had developed by listening to people who didn't know me. I found that sharing my feelings and accepting help from those who cared was the best medicine for me.

You must always try to be the best person you are capable of being, and be happy with that person. No one is perfect. I am sure there are many other kids who have the same problem I did. My advice to them: Believe in yourself and accept help if you need it. Talking to someone will make you feel a lot better. It did for me. Most of all, remember you are not alone, ever. There is always someone there for you.

Being Overweight

....

Jessica Haynes, age 12

HI. MY NAME IS JESSICA HAYNES AND I AM FAT. PEOPLE
may think I don't try to lose weight, but I do. I've tried
swimming, dieting, and even throwing up after I eat.

When I was in second grade, I realized I was much bigger than other kids my age. I liked a boy in my class, but I
figured he would never like me because I was fat. The kids
always made fun of me because of my weight. When my
school had a party, I would never eat any of the cookies or
drink any soda because I didn't want to be teased. Kids in
my class, especially the boys, would tease me. When I
walked by, they would pretend that I caused an earth-
quake. They called me Porky Pig, Elephant, and Whale.

When I was in third grade, it got a little better. I was
still teased, but I tried to ignore it. It still hurt a lot inside.
There were days when I came home in tears and I wouldn't
want to go to school the next day. I hoped and prayed
every night that I would wake up thin.

When I was in fourth grade, we started swimming at
our school. I knew how to swim very well. I swam better
than any of the girls in my class. When one of the boys

asked, "Who's the best girl swimmer?" I replied modestly, "Me." All the boys began to laugh as if what I had said was a big joke. One boy, still laughing hysterically said, "You can swim because you're a whale."

I was ashamed. I had so much anger in me, I began to cry. A teacher came and asked me why I was crying. I told her the boys were making fun of me and she comforted me.

When my mother and I would go shopping at the mall, I would be very embarrassed to eat at a fast-food restaurant. I felt like people were looking at me and saying, "She shouldn't eat that."

In sixth grade, I had a very insensitive teacher. One day she told the entire class that we were going to dance on stage for the whole school. Some girls were not going to dance because the dance teacher only had eleven costumes. None of them were big enough to fit my best friend or me. We were allowed to audition, but neither of us were selected. We were very disappointed. We said that we didn't care, but I did. The next day, I could not bear to go to school because I wanted to be in the dance so badly.

Two summers ago, when I was at the doctor's office, my mom looked at my chart. It said I weighed 178 pounds. My mom was very angry. She told me that I had to get thinner. I tried everything. I starved myself and took diet pills, but it didn't work.

This summer was a turning point for me. I realized that pills and starving myself were not the answer. Now I try to eat a healthy diet. I have learned to express myself. I'm a good person and I'm okay just the way I am. I realize that kids can be cruel sometimes. If they say unkind things, it's because they don't feel good about themselves.

I hope that by writing this essay I can help other people who have a weight problem. I have more confidence now, and that's why I can write about it. I know that in order for people to like you, you have to like yourself. Sometimes it's hard to change how you look, but you can change the way you feel about your appearance. I did.

PROBLEM RESOLUTION

The Petition

....

Nicole Starr, age 12

IN THE SIXTH GRADE, INTRAMURAL HOCKEY WAS BEGIN-
ning. My friends and I signed up. When we were making
up teams, we noticed that we had to play with the fourth
and fifth graders. The boys didn't have to play with the
fourth- and fifth-grade boys; they got to play with the
other sixth graders. I didn't think this was fair, so I told my
parents. They said that I should write a petition.

About a day later, I started the petition, even though
the gym teacher had already made up the schedule. I got
everybody in my class to sign it, even my teacher. As he
signed it, he said, "It probably won't make a difference
because the coach already made up the teams and schedules." My friend Jessica wasn't going to sign it, because she
thought it might get her in trouble. I said, "Jes, do you
really want to play with the younger kids? Wouldn't you
rather play with the people in our grade?"

"Of course," she said. "Why would I want to play with
the fourth and fifth graders?"

"If you don't want to play with them, why don't you
sign it?" I exclaimed.

"Well, okay, I guess you're right," Jessica said.

Another teammate was in a different class, so I gave her the petition so she could get signatures from her class. She got almost everybody, except her teacher. The teacher said she wouldn't sign it because it was our fight and she wanted us to win it by ourselves.

After school, we had gathered about forty signatures. We saw some more kids on the playground. They agreed with us that it wasn't fair, so they signed it. Now we had about fifty-five people.

The next day, I had gym class. Our coach wasn't there, so I left the petition laying on his desk, hoping it wouldn't fall off.

That next week in gym class, the coach didn't say anything. I guessed he had gotten the petition, because the next day during our reading time, the teachers passed out the new teams and new schedules. I was so excited. My parents' plan had worked. The coach changed his mind because of my parents, my friends, and me. In fact, when it came time for basketball intramurals, he made the teams with the sixth graders together.

I was happy that I'd been able to change something at my school. Even though it was a little change, it made the girls feel a lot better, plus my hockey team finished as number 1 or 2.

From doing this petition, I realized that if you really want and believe in something, you have to get it yourself. You have to stand up for what you believe in. It is important to know that no matter what your age, you really can make a difference if you go about it in a peaceful way. If you want to make changes, think of what you can do in your life to make things better not only for yourself, but for others.

Good and Bad

....

K.T., age 9

WHEN I WAS LITTLE, MY MOTHER AND FATHER SPLIT UP. I don't really remember it, but now I see my dad every other weekend because I live with my mom.

I was lonely in my old hometown, but since I've moved to my new town, I've made a lot of friends. One of my best friends is Stacey. It wasn't always easy to make friends. I was the new kid, and the worst experience I had was with the first friend I made. We were friends for a while, but then she moved away. I was sad, but I made more friends eventually.

I met this nice girl across the street from where I live. Her name is Jenna. She is really nice and I like her a lot. We wanted to play together during the day, but my mom worked. That meant I had to go to daycare. My mom took me to the YMCA and said that the people there would take care of me while she worked. When I first went there, I was scared and started to cry. My mom said, "Look, there is Jenna playing with her Legos!" I was both surprised and happy. I ran over to start playing with her. We were good friends then, and we still are today.

Friends can come in all shapes and sizes. I've learned that. One of my very best friends now is my cat, Disney. He is very nice to me. Some animals are not so nice. I know all about that! Once, when I was little, I got bit in the face by a dog. It was pretty serious and my parents had to rush me to the hospital. I am lucky that I still have my eye because I was bitten very close to my eye. I think about that a lot, but I know that animals are a lot like people. Some are really nice and friendly and some are not. The older I get, the better I'm getting at telling the two apart.

School for me has been pretty good. I've been to a lot of schools and have had a lot of different teachers. In kindergarten, I had the nicest teacher in the world. People say I was lucky to have her, and I think they're right. I remember doing cool things in school like sending goodies to the soldiers in Bosnia and making a lot more friends. Now I'm in fourth grade, and my teacher is very, very nice. She knows I'm trying hard, and I'm smarter now than I have ever been. I know she is proud of me and I love her.

So, you can see that even though I'm nine years old, I've had a lot of experiences. Some have been good, and some not so good, but I've learned that most of the stuff that happens to me is good, so even when it's going bad I just keep remembering the good times and wait for the good things to start happening all over again!

A Smile Is a Sweet Reward

Morgan Newton, age 12

THE AREA I LIVE IN IS PRETTY NICE MOST OF THE TIME.
I live five blocks away from a playground and baseball
diamond.

This summer we got a newsletter from the police warning us to keep our bikes locked up at night and out of
sight when we are not with them. There had been a lot of
bike robberies, even though the summer had just begun.

Karen, my fourteen-year-old sister, and I panted as we
neared the end of our mile run. During our run, we saw
Tim and a couple of other guys at the park. On our way
back, we saw them go down Terry's street. Terry is twelve,
just like me. When we started heading back home, we saw
Terry frantically looking around. She told us that Jason, a
kid across the street from her, got a brand new black bike
he had been saving up to buy. He went across the street to
show off his dream bike to some friends. They were on the
front porch playing Legos when some guys came up right
in front of him and stole his bike!

Karen and I quickly ran home, hopped on our bikes, and started looking for Tim and his friends. We suspected they were the culprits. We looked where Karen had seen them before—on Terry's street. There we saw Jason. Karen and I described Tim and asked if he was the one who stole his bike. Jason told us that he was wearing the same clothes we described and had brown hair plastered to his head, just like Tim.

The police arrived shortly after Jason's baby-sitter called them. The police officer questioned the boys who saw the robber. He searched for a while, but didn't come up with anything. While the officer looked around, my mom came by and gave Terry, Karen, and me a ride in our van. We looked around but when we found Tim, half of his friends were gone and no one had the bike. Tim yelled, "Hey, what's up?" But we ignored him and kept driving.

After we had seen Tim and his friends, we turned around and started driving the way they had just come. We went behind the Subway restaurant and looked for the bicycle. We went over to see if they had stashed it anywhere. We looked in dumpsters but had no luck. What we did find was a big, white, five-gallon bucket filled with vomit and a torn bike seat. We kept looking.

We finally gave up and headed back home with heavy feet, sweaty bodies, and hungry stomachs. At home, our spirits lifted as we told Jason what we had found. Then, a light bulb went off in my head. We could look in a yearbook and find the guys who stole the bikes. Then we could call them.

We found the guys in the yearbook and their phone numbers in the phone book. Then we left to get ready for the Neighborhood Watch party we were hosting. During the party, Jason's dad called Tim and demanded that the bike be placed in his front yard within twenty minutes or he would call the police. In fifteen minutes, the bike had been returned. Everyone cheered!

It takes teamwork and patience to achieve the sweet rewards of life. After you have willingly given your share of time and effort, you will come to see that the joy in a person's face is your reward. This thankfulness is even better than a twenty-speed bike.

My Bike and Me

Brian Osborne, age 8

I LOVE MY BIKE. IT'S RED AND GREEN, AND I TAKE GOOD care of it. I feel free riding my bike. I can ride really fast—ten miles an hour!—and do big wheelies on the street. I help my sister ride fast like me. My sister has a mountain bike.

One day I rode my bike around the block. I was going so fast I felt lots of wind as I watched the pretty houses speed by. It was fun. My friend and I were riding safely on the street. After a while, I went home and played a game. I was taking a break from my bike.

The next day, I went outside and played with my sister. Then I went around the block to get my friend. Alan and I played Mario Kart 64. We had fun at first. Later, I didn't have much fun because I was worried about my sister. I decided to go look for her. When I went to look for my bike, it wasn't where I had left it. Then I saw my sister at the gang house, so I went over there. The gang was bossing me and my sister. They had stolen my bike. I was mad. In a way, they stole my freedom by stealing my bike.

The gang was bigger and stronger than I was, and my sister and I were having a hard time. The gang teased us and hurt me on the street. I ran home and told my mom that the gang was being mean and tried to steal my bike. My mom got really mad and went around the block to speak to them. She almost got into a fight with them, but I stopped her. My sister was really mad at the gang. I was lucky to get her home. I solved the problem by talking instead of fighting.

I don't ride around the block anymore. Instead, I ride in a different direction. So far, everything has been fine. I hope it stays that way. It's great to have a bike to ride on and to go just about anywhere you want to go. From my experience, I'd say it's better to talk it out when you have a problem rather than argue or fight. If every kid did that, we would have a peaceful world to live in.

Too Much Pressure

....

Alicia, age 12

HAVE YOU EVER HAD TOO MUCH PRESSURE FROM PARENTS, teachers, coaches, or your friends? Have you ever had so much pressure that it made you sick, literally, so that you had to miss school? I have. I got sick from pressure I actually built up myself.

One thing that triggered all of this sickness was sports. I played soccer and basketball at the same time. Big deal, right? Well, it was a big deal for me because I wasn't just playing with one team. I was playing with three indoor teams. I also played with an outdoor program called ODP (Olympic Development Program). With this team, all the players were one year older, so I got knocked around a lot.

My two indoor teams were very organized. We had plenty of subs and things ran smoothly. The problem with the other indoor team was that our coach wanted to be undefeated. He threatened to make us run back and forth across the field if we lost. Good thing we never lost. But right there, it was already too much pressure for me.

I kept pushing myself to be the best, so I signed up for ODP. I was traveling to Dayton every Wednesday. We played outdoor games a lot, so we would get colds and stuff. Most nights I had ODP practice, then a soccer game, then a basketball game. I usually wouldn't get home until about 10:30.

Basketball was also pretty trying. We had two games a week, with practice twice a week. The pressure for basketball wouldn't have been so great except that all my friends, including my boyfriend at the time, came to all of the games. So I had to do well in practices to impress my friends. Whenever I had spare time, which wasn't often, I practiced basketball at the hoop in front of our house.

Then there was school. My teacher was probably the hardest, but greatest, teacher in the whole county. Of course, when all of these sports were going on, so were the proficiencies.

Our teacher wanted our sixth-grade class to have the highest scores, so she taught us nonstop during the day and gave us a tremendous amount of homework. Every night she would give us a twenty-five-page story to read, and then we would have to write a book report about it. She gave us two lessons in math so we would know more than we had to, just in case. Then we had a book with all these different writing assignments, and every night we would have to do a different assignment. We had to do a prewrite, sloppy copy, and then a final draft. That took forever. Of course, I wanted to get a good grade so I tried to do the best I could.

Now, that is a lot of homework to do, but to do it all in one night is almost impossible. But I had to impress my parents and my teacher.

A normal teenager would just skip the homework and half of the sports and say the heck with it. But if you lived in my family, you wouldn't. My mom expects so much from me when it comes to school, because no one else in the family did that well in school. I'm the youngest. I'm their only hope, or so they say. My sister never pays attention in class, she just sits there and daydreams the whole time. Plus, she never does her homework. My brother is pretty smart, he just doesn't apply himself.

So, if you add all this stuff up, it's way too much, especially for an eleven year old. But somehow I managed. Every night I would go to bed at midnight and get up the next morning at 6:30 to finish my homework, then my stressful day would start all over again.

After doing all of this, you begin to have a feeling of despair. You begin to believe that everyone is pressuring you to do everything, even though they're not. I began to think that everyone was on my case 24-7. I dumped my boyfriend because I thought I didn't deserve him. At the time, I was yelling at all my friends, so they were mostly always mad at me. School and sports were my life, and it felt like the world was ending.

When you start to feel this way, you begin to feel sick from all of the pressure, and that's what happened to me. First my throat started to hurt; I could barely even talk. Then I started getting these pounding headaches. I think it was because I never got much sleep. When this started to happen, my grades began to slip and my athletic ability declined.

I didn't tell my parents until I got a stomachache along with my headache and sore throat. Still, I kept pushing myself until the day my mom made me stay home from school. When she did, I started to cry. I guess I couldn't take all the pressure.

I was out of school for a total of twenty-two days. I laid off the sports for a while, and I realized that nobody cared if I didn't win a soccer game or if I made every basket that I shot. Everybody just wanted me to take care of myself.

To this day, I still sometimes feel that massive block of pressure building up inside my head. Whenever I feel this happening, I take a deep breath and tell myself that I don't have to be perfect, that it doesn't matter because not everything is my responsibility. I wrote this not only to help myself understand what happened, but also to make other kids my age realize how one's thinking can take over one's mind and body. Remember to take it one step at a time, and know that everything is not your fault. Remember that you're just a little kid, struggling to be someone or something in the world.

School

First Day of School

Jennifer, age 10

WHEN I FIRST STARTED GOING TO SCHOOL, I WAS SCARED that the other kids might laugh at me. I had never been to school before, and I didn't really know what to think. I remember when I first saw my classroom I felt bad and started to cry. I instantly knew I wanted my mom, but when I looked back, my mom was gone. Being in a strange place, I wasn't sure everyone was friendly, and now that my mom had gone, I started to cry even more. My teacher came to me and kindly told me that everything was going to be fine. That didn't help right away, but after a while I felt better about being there.

Having a kind teacher and friends who were nice to me on my first day of school makes this memory a good one. If you ask me what I learned on my first day of school, I'd tell you that even though you're in a new place doing something you never did before, and it's uncomfortable, if you look for kind faces and be yourself, it'll be all right. Kind faces and loving acts can make everything around you seem a little better.

Wrong School

Zac Whitney, age 7

I HAD A PROBLEM. I WAS IN THE WRONG SCHOOL, THE wrong grade, and with the wrong teacher. That may not seem like a big problem, but no matter what I did, I got in trouble. I went to kindergarten for a second year. It was so totally easy that it stunk. I had thought that if I repeated kindergarten it would be a good idea. The grownups said kindergarten was really fun, but—hello!—kindergarten is boring the second time around! The school promised that I would stay with the same teacher. Her name was Linda. At that school, teachers go by their first names. I liked Linda as a teacher. She was nice and I felt liked by her. The problem started when they moved the teacher. I was mad. My class was so easy—they were teaching "two plus two"; I wanted to learn technology. They were reading books for young kids, and I wanted to read things like Usborne's *The Pyramid Plot.*

I went to the office at least once a day for doing things like having fun and doing nothing. Once, the teacher said I could come back to the room, but I said no, I wanted to stay in the office for the rest of the day. Seemed to me like a good way to solve the problem. I felt like an idiot. I was stuck in kindergarten and I kept going around saying, "I hate school" and "I hate life." I was angry, upset—all the mad words. I was called "the bad kid" in my class. Oh, yeah, and no one invited me to their birthday parties or to their houses to play. I knew the answers in school, but I felt like everybody else must have known the answers, too. I kept going around saying, "Duh, everybody knows that." I felt dumb because I always got in trouble. Even when my mom said she'd buy me a toy if I could stay out of the office, I still couldn't stop getting into trouble.

I tried to fix it all by running out the door at school. That got me into big trouble. They kicked me out of school that day, and my mom had to skip her school to take care of me. We sat on the couch and talked and cried. That was all there was to do.

I kept my feelings inside and they gave me stomachaches and headaches. I used to cry in bed and beg not to go to school. I would try to amuse myself at school by reading in the corner, and I tried going to a doctor. That didn't help.

Things began to change when I started going to the resource teacher. That was really fun. He let me play hard and easy games on the computer. He had books I could read and take back to my room. My grandma came and I got to come home early. She and I read the backs of cereal boxes and saw how much salt each cereal had. I got to play outside and even do a little bit of gardening with Grandma. (She loves gardening.) I usually got up and said

"Yahoo!" when my mom or dad said grandma would come to get me from school. I took some tests, some with the resource teacher and some with the school psychologist. Some were with a woman who sounded like she was from England. She was very nice. I remember one of the tests. I had to put things in order, but I passed it easily. One test was drawing pictures and telling about my feelings. The man asked me why I didn't put any mouths on my pictures—I usually drew superheroes. I just said, "I never do." I went to see an occupational therapist and she tested my muscles and my writing. Once the tests were done, I ended up changing schools.

Man, was I scared. I thought my new school would be just like my old one. I was scared that I would be sent to the office every single day. I was scared I would feel the same way, even though my mom and dad told me not to worry. They said it would be okay. The first day I met my teacher, Ms. Matala. I was sort of scared, but I thought she was going to be a pretty good teacher. She was nice. She showed me around and gave me the job of computer manager.

My new school is hard, but in a good way—it makes my brain work. We have a computer in the room, and we have a computer lab with fifty computers! I like my teacher because she smiles, likes computers and math, and tells us jokes. It was hard to make friends at first, but now I have a few. My other teacher teaches about anger control, feelings, science, and geography. She lets me take my tests verbally, and last time I got the only 100 percent in my whole class! My handwriting has gotten better—I can write three sentences if I want. I've learned to type on the computer pretty well, too.

I skipped first grade and am now in second. I started going to karate to build my muscles. I get to let out all my anger on pads, people with pads on, and the air. My parents gave me a gift certificate for karate, and now I go twice a week. I'm a green belt now.

I have learned that when I have a problem I can go to a resource teacher. I have learned that changing schools can make a big difference. I have learned to tell my parents when I'm really miserable, and they can help because they love me and want me to be happy. Parents aren't the only grownups who can help, though. Your teacher—that only applies if your teacher doesn't hate you, but teachers usually like their students—grandparents, and the boss of the school can all get involved to help. My mom and dad said their taxes pay for these people.

This year, I laugh a lot more. I can tell my parents anything. (I even told my mom that my dad is my favorite parent now and she took it well.) I have learned to like my learning style because I can read better than anybody in my class. I think I understand math more than most people in my class, and I am easy to encourage because I've had a lot of practice. Say I start doing something and then my mom comes and says, "Come on, let's do something else," and I say, "Oh man, why can't I just keep doing what

I'm doing?" and then if I don't have to do it, I can just keep doing what I'm doing. I've been like that ever since I was born. Once I started sleeping I wouldn't want to wake up, but if I'm awake, I don't want to go to sleep. I don't like changing unless my conditions fit what that thing is—this is part of my learning style.

My problem started last school year. I hadn't had a problem before that, but last year it was a pretty big problem. I thought there was something wrong with me. Now I realize it wasn't me—it was the school being the wrong school for me that was the problem. By changing schools, I was able to overcome the problem.

NOTE:

In kindergarten, Zac was diagnosed with giftedness as well as a significant learning disability: Non Verbal Learning Disorder. His test scores show that his vocabulary and language skills are consistent with a twelfth grader's, his math and reading are at a fourth- or fifth-grade level, but his ability to perform skills such as handwriting, organization, and dealing with social cues are up to three years delayed. Zac wants to be a cartoonist and a scientist when he grows up and is currently collaborating with a grownup to write a screen play about James Bond. He also has started drawing a series of comic frames in hopes of having the first action hero comic in his local paper.

Asking for Help

Gill Carroll, age 12

THIS IS A TRUE STORY ABOUT ME, MY PARENTS, AND MY grades.

It all started a year ago in the state of Washington. My family had moved there over the summer. Although I enjoyed going to school there, Washington's education system was not as challenging for me as Ohio's was, no offense intended. My teacher was very good at what she did, but we rarely had any homework, and the little that we did receive was not very difficult. As a result, that year of school was really sort of easy. But the summer of 1997 brought us back to Ohio, and the beginning of this school year showed that things were going to be very different.

My parents were upset with me, and voices were getting loud. My mom was all alone because my dad was out of town on business—but you can bet I heard about it from him over the phone. Their usual straight-A student had received a D in English, a C in social studies, and a B+ in Spanish. I was very upset with my grades and with myself. Fortunately for me, my bad grades were mostly due to a few assignments given while I was absent.

I sat on my bed in bewilderment, feeling haggard and spattered with disgust. My parents and I both knew that I could do much better. We knew that I could set and achieve higher goals.

I was in a pitiable state, and I knew it. I thought of how nice it would be to have caring, soothing friends to guide me through this situation. Little did I know that my parents would be these friends.

They came right out and told me as much. They told me that they were disappointed about my grades, but then they talked about it with me. We sat down at the kitchen table and talked about the situation. As I said before, my poor grades were partly the result of an absence. I knew I could make up the work and get full credit. Some of my grades, however, were from tests I did not study for, and now I was suffering the consequences of enjoying free nights when I should have been studying.

My dad gave me the same speech about three different times because I just sat there and said nothing. He told me it was important to share problems and feelings with each other. He also told me that they were fighting for me, not against me. I continued to sit there and didn't say a single word. After that, he was so fed up that he made me stay in my room until I would tell them what was wrong.

Finally, as you might imagine, I flew the white flag and they won. I'm glad they won. I told them about how the difference between the Washington and Ohio school systems was causing me a great deal of trouble and confusion. But I promised to improve. It felt really good to spit it out to someone else and discuss it.

Next, we needed a plan. My parents and I worked on this by checking my plan book every night. I remember them asking me daily about any problems at school and if everything was all right. My dad was concerned, he would repeatedly ask how things were going.

My parents and I are now working together. I share all the news, good and bad, with them. There's no more holding back and pushing in opposite directions. We—and I do mean we—are making my grades go up faster than anything you've ever seen.

I now have an A in social studies, English, and Spanish. I've learned that you should always check your work and do your best, because you never know what you can do. I have also learned that you need to express your feelings, even if you think they are a little odd or uncool. I've learned that your parents are pushing for you and not against you.

I'm very glad of this achievement and have thanked my mom and dad for their help and for everything they give to me. Other kids should learn from this essay that they should always study, ask for help when they need it, and never, ever, think that they are too cool for anything. This includes their parents, other kids, and school. They should also learn that they need to express their feelings like I did. Finally, they should remember that their parents are there for them, instead of against them.

DIVERSITY

Friends

....

Irene, age 11

EVERY WEEKDAY MORNING I WAKE UP, BRUSH MY TEETH, and take a shower to get ready for school. I go to elementary school and I'm in fifth grade. My favorite thing to do is to play basketball. I am on a basketball team. My favorite foods are Reese's Pieces, brownies, sweets, and Italian food. I have an older brother and a younger sister. I am one of the few African Americans at my school, and that's something that makes me special.

Most of my friends are white. One of my best friends is Jewish and from South Africa. I have learned that one of her religious celebrations is to have a get-together on certain Fridays with family and friends. At these gatherings they say a Jewish prayer and then eat. In addition to learning about her religion, I have tried different types of foods at her house, including Challah, a type of bread. She also has shown me different things from South Africa, such as rock paper weights. They are beautiful.

Susan, another friend, is from Pakistan. Her family celebrates Ramadan, during which her family fasts. Susan's brother is too young to fast, and Susan only fasts on weekends. They also hang meat in their garage for Ramadan.

Kate is my blonde-haired, green-eyed, Christian friend from Louisiana. We're best friends. I went to her baptism and attended her church for a while. Last summer I went on vacation with Kate and her family. We visited her grandmother. Our families are like one big family.

There are advantages and disadvantages to going to a mostly white school. An advantage is that I have been introduced to many types of music, religion, and even clothing styles. Before I moved here, I had never heard of musical groups such as Sublime and Sugar Ray. Nor had I ever heard of singers like Robyn, Celine Dion, or Meredith Brooks. Inco Jeans and Ramadan were also new to me.

A disadvantage of going to a mostly white school is that when I do something like relax or braid my hair, some of my friends think it's sort of weird. Also, sometimes I feel as if I'm alone because I have tastes that differ from some of my friends. I feel that my friend Kate understands me the most because we have similar tastes. That's why she's my best friend.

I have learned that no matter what race a person is, their parents want the best for them, just as your parents do, and education is important. Other children should know that you shouldn't judge people by the color of their skin, and having a diverse group of friends is noteworthy.

I have learned about many different cultures and tried many types of food because of my friends. Even though something may seem gross to you, it may not be to someone else—and it could actually turn out to be great. Although most of my friends are white, I know that everyone should like each other for who they are and not judge them merely by the color of their skin.

Aaron and Me

....

Kelley Marie Oberne, age 10

LAST YEAR, MY BROTHER AND I WERE TAKING SWIMMING lessons at the Northside Swimming Pool in Norfolk. Our mother was late and we were tired of waiting on the bench outside. We heard lots of kids having fun at the nearby park. We really wanted to swing on one of the swing sets and go down the slides. So, we went over there hoping to have some fun.

I have to walk slowly, so my older brother can keep up with me. Aaron was in a car accident when he was two years old. He is different from other kids, but so am I. Aaron is kind of chubby and has a hard time tying his shoes. He can't use his hands like I can and he's not quick like I am. But he's really smart. He can read encyclopedias and do math problems in his head. I have trouble with reading because my eyes are weak. I take eye drops for them. My mom says that I have glaucoma and need to wear my sunglasses when I'm playing outside. When I have trouble seeing something, Aaron always helps me.

Well, today the sun was real hot and it was hurting my eyes. I didn't have my sunglasses, so I sat in the shade. Aaron went over to one of the swing sets.

There were lots of bushes where I was sitting and I picked some yellow flowers and leaves. I was going to make a pretty bouquet for my mom. I saw a group of boys pass by. There were eight of them. They must have been teenagers. They were bigger than I was. In fact, they were taller than Aaron, and he was twelve years old. They were swearing and spitting at each other. They went over to the swing set that Aaron was on. I saw Aaron get off his swing. One of the big boys pushed Aaron down. When Aaron tried to get up, one of the boys hit him with his fist. Aaron's nose started to bleed. Well, that made me really mad!

Aaron wasn't doing anything to them. I ran over there and told those boys to leave my brother alone. They just laughed at me, so I did the only thing that came naturally—I lied. Everyone says that I am a great actress. I told those rotten boys that my father was a sumo wrestler and there he was. I pointed to a real fat guy coming out of the swimming pool building. The boys believed me and took off running. I saw dust flying behind them.

I helped Aaron up. I ran over and got his wet towel and placed it on his face. We walked to a bench and sat down. It seemed like forever before our mom arrived, but actually she was only ten minutes late.

The worst part about what happened to Aaron was that it took him a long time before he went back to the park to play. Mom and Dad took us to a different park to play, but it just wasn't that much fun. Aaron would go down the slides, but he wouldn't get on the swings. Then, one day, Aaron went on one of the swings. He said he was tired of the slides. The next week, we went back to Northside Park. We thought Aaron was finally over his fear. We were wrong. Aaron only sat on one of the benches and looked around. I told Aaron that Mom and Dad were with us and nothing would happen if the boys showed up.

There was a lady clown in the park that day. She made animals out of balloons. She made a poodle for me and a bear for Aaron. It was a little windy and Aaron's balloon started to fly away. It ended up near one of the swings. Aaron grabbed his balloon bear and sat on one of the swings. I decided to sit next to Aaron with my balloon poodle. We made up names for our animals. He called his Balloonie and I called mine Sunny. We had a lot of fun that day.

I learned a lot about myself from that experience. I can keep calm in a tragic situation while helping someone else. When I grow up, I'm going to be a nurse or an emergency medical technician. Everyone needs to be responsible for the things they do and the things they say. We need to realize that we are all different and unique in some special way. All of us need to appreciate our differences because that's what makes us who we are.

Our Panel of Judges

MAYOR NORM COLEMAN

Norm Coleman was elected to his second term as mayor of St. Paul, Minnesota. Prior to this, he served seventeen years in the Minnesota Attorney General's office and was the state's Solicitor General and Chief Prosecutor.

MARLY CORNELL

Marly Cornell is a social justice activist, artist, and writer who has worked twenty-four years in healthcare. Her drawings and paintings have been commissioned by organizations such as Primarily Primates, CEASE, and the Animal Rights Coalition. She has written for various publications, including *The Animal's AGENDA,* where she served for several years as a contributing editor. Marly has traveled world-wide to speak at many universities about her work. Currently, she is the chair of the Ethics Committee for the Institute for Chemical Dependency Professionals, a contributor to the Speakers Bureau of the Animal Rights Coalition, and a member of the advisory committee for Fairview Press. Marly lives in St. Louis Park, Minnesota.

Senator Rod Grams

Senator Rod Grams (R-Minnesota) was sworn in as a member of the United States Senate on January 4, 1995. He serves on several Senate committees, and, in 1996, he was appointed by President Clinton to serve as a Congressional Delegate to the 51st Session of the United Nations General Assembly. Prior to his governmental service, Senator Grams spent twenty-three years in the field of television and radio broadcasting.

Linda Hillyer

Linda Hillyer is a writer, editor, peer counselor, and disability activist. She is currently compiling an anthology of personal and creative expressions by young people with disabilities entitled *Listen to Our Stories: Words, Pictures, and Songs by Kids with Disabilities.*

Nkauj'lis Lyfoung

Nkauj'lis Lyfoung is currently the Project Coordinator for *Don't Believe the Hype* at Channel 2/17, Twin Cities Public Television. She got her break in the television industry by working on *Kev Koom Siab,* the first Hmong television program produced by PBS. Nkauj'lis is also the co-founder of Pom Siab Hmoob Theatre, the first professional Hmong theatre in the USA, and is an actor, director, and playwright. In 1993, she won an Asian American Academic Achievement Award from her alma mater, the University of Minnesota. Along with performing, writing, and grassroots organizing, Nkauj'lis has also served on numerous panel discussions and has been a representative to national conferences that deal with youth issues.

KATHLEEN PAPATOLA

Kathleen J. Papatola, Ph.D., graduated from the University of British Columbia, Vancouver, Canada, in 1982. She is a Licensed Psychologist with fifteen years of clinical experience. In addition to her clinical work, Dr. Papatola consults with organizations, trains mental health providers, and engages in public speaking. She is the author of *The Therapy Answer Book: Getting the Most out of Counseling* and writes a regular column on current psychological issues for the *St. Paul Pioneer Press'* Opinion Page.

HERTICENA SELF

Herticena was a teacher and principal in the Minneapolis Public Schools for twenty-seven years. After retiring from Minneapolis in 1992, she joined the College of Education at the University of Minnesota as Director of the K–12 outreach programs. She retired from the U of M in 1998. Presently, Herticena is an Educational Consultant providing continuing professional development training for administrators in urban cities.

ROBYN FREEDMAN SPIZMAN

The author of more than sixty parenting, educational, and "how-to" books, Robyn Freedman Spizman and her husband co-own The Spizman Agency in Atlanta, Georgia, which specializes in media and public relations. Robyn has appeared for the past fifteen years as "Super Mom," a consumer advocate on NBC WXIA-TV's *Noonday*. A former art educator and a mother of two, Robyn's parenting advice has been featured on CNN, CNBC, and The Discovery Channel, and in numerous publications including *Family Circle, Reader's Digest, Parents Magazine, Child, USA Today,* and *Better Homes and Gardens.*

Other Resources for Young People from Fairview Press

The Body by Slim Goodbody. ISBN 0-925190-85-3, hardcover, 8 x 10, 48 pages, $15.95. Skin, muscles, bones, digestion, and much more are examined through fun rhymes, detailed diagrams, amazing facts, healthy advice, and simple experiments. Ages 3–9.

Born Early: A Premature Baby's Story by Lida Lafferty and Bo Flood, photographs by Rebecca Young. ISBN 1-57749-064-9, paperback, 7 x 10, 48 pages, $9.95. This award-winning book follows a baby from her premature birth to her homecoming, explaining the many medical procedures that take place in a neonatal intensive care unit in a hospital. All ages.

Box-Head Boy: Helping Kids Cope with Too Much TV by Christine M. Winn, with David Walsh, PhD. ISBN 0-925190-88-8, hardcover, 8 x 10, 32 pages, $14.95. When nine-year-old Denny watches too much television, he becomes a "box-head boy." At first this seems like a dream come true, but when he discovers he can't move or speak in his television world, he has to figure out a way back to the real world. Ages 3–9.

Brave New Girls: Creative Ideas to Help Girls Be Confident, Healthy, and Happy by Jeanette Gadeberg. ISBN 1-57749-049-5, paperback 7 x 10, 192 pages, $12.95. A hands-on, straight-talking guide for helping girls deal with family relationships, body image, money management, sexual harassment, and much more. Ages 8–13.

Clover's Secret: Helping Kids Cope with Domestic Violence by Christine M. Winn, with David Walsh, PhD. ISBN 0-925190-89-6, hardcover, 8 x 10, 32 pages, $14.95. Shy Clover and outgoing Micky seem like opposites, but they become good friends and flying buddies in the imaginary village of Woobie. In a dramatic discovery, Mickey learns that Clover's home is troubled by violence. Ages 3–9.

The Cycle of Life by Slim Goodbody. ISBN 1-57749-050-9, hardcover, 8 x 10, 48 pages. Memorable rhymes and interesting facts teach kids about the cycles of life in nature: being born, growing up, growing old, and dying. Ages 3–9.

Help Me Say Goodbye: Activities for Helping Kids Cope When a Special Person Dies by Janis Silverman. ISBN 1-57749-085-1, paperback, 10 x 7, 32 pages, $6.95. An art therapy and activity book for young children coping with the death of someone they love. Ages 3–9.

How We Made the World a Better Place: Kids and Teens Write on How They Changed Their Corner of the World by Fairview Press. ISBN 1-57749-079-7, paperback, 6 x 9, 160 pages,

$9.95. Essays by kids and teens who have made a difference in the world. All ages.

Hurry, Murray, Hurry! by Bob Keeshan. ISBN 0-925190-84-5, hardcover, 8 x 10, 32 pages, $14.95. In a fast-paced world where children are told to hurry up, two third-grade friends demonstrate how to enjoy life by taking it at a reasonable pace. Also available in Spanish. Ages 5–10.

I'll Go to School If . . . by Bo Flood. ISBN 1-57749-024-X, hardcover, 8 $^{3/4}$ x 8 $^{3/4}$, 32 pages, $14.95. "I'll go to school if . . . I can ride on the back of a lion!" This imaginative declaration masks the fear a boy feels about his first day of school. He discovers, though, that his mother is just as apprehensive, and helping her gives him the courage he needs to face his fear. Ages 2–6.

The Mind by Slim Goodbody. ISBN 1-57749-020-7, hardcover, 8 x 10, $14.95. Fascinating facts and helpful diagrams explain how and why the brain works. Explore the mind's inseparable connection with the rest of the body, and learn about the everyday activities of the mind—imagination, creativity, memory, and much more. Ages 3–9.

Monster Boy: Helping Kids Cope with Anger by Christine M. Winn, with David Walsh, PhD. ISBN 0-925190-87-X, hardcover, 8 x 10, 32 pages, $14.95. Hot-head Buster meets a monster, and matches it shout for shout and stomp for stomp until his temper tantrum turns him into a monster, too! Ages 3–9.

My Dad Has HIV by Earl Alexander, Sheila Rudin, and Pam Sejkora. ISBN 0-925190-99-3, hardcover, 8 x 10, 32 pages, $14.95. This groundbreaking book relates the facts about HIV and AIDS in a sensitive and positive way that children can understand. Ages 2–8.

Naomi Wants to Know: Letters from a Little Girl to the Big Big World by Naomi Shavin. ISBN 1-57749-076-2, paperback, 7 x 10, 160 pages, $12.95. A six-year-old's correspondence with famous and interesting people around the world. All ages.

Sisters, Brothers, and Disabilities: A Family Album by Lydia Gans. ISBN 1-57749-044-4, paperback, 8 x 9, 160 pages, $12.95. Photoessay telling the stories of twenty-six families raising children with special needs along with their brothers and sisters. All ages.

The Spirit by Slim Goodbody. ISBN 1-57749-016-9, hardcover, 8 x 10, 32 pages, $14.95. Readers explore the ideas of doing right, accepting personal values, being true to one's self, learning from mistakes, and appreciating one's self. Ages 3–9.

Teens Write Through It: Essays from Teens Who Have Triumphed Over Trouble by Fairview Press. ISBN 1-57749-083-5, paperback, 6 x 9, 224 pages, $9.95. Essays by teens who have overcome a challenge in their lives. All ages.

To order, call toll-free 1-800-544-8207